SENSE ABOUT DEFENCE

Publication of this extremely important document is both a contribution to the widespread debate about defence as well as a demonstration of ways in which the massive defence burden can be reduced.

Aspects covered in the book, such as the economic implications of cuts, the creation of new jobs and the arms trade are of interest to all of us. New and important light is thrown on all these areas in a lucid and readable form.

SENSE ABOUT DEFENCE
The Report of the Labour Party
Defence Study Group

Foreword by Ron Hayward

Introduction by Ian Mikardo, MP

QUARTET BOOKS
LONDON   MELBOURNE   NEW YORK

First published by Quartet Books Limited 1977
A member of the Namara Group
27 Goodge Street, London W1P 1FD

Copyright © 1977 by The Labour Party
Labour Party stock code: B/028/09/77

ISBN 0 7043 3194 2

Typesetting by Bedford Typesetters Limited

Printed and bound in Great Britain by
The Garden City Press Limited
Letchworth, Hertfordshire SG6 1JS

CONTENTS

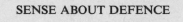
SENSE ABOUT DEFENCE

FOREWORD

by Ron Hayward
General Secretary, The Labour Party

The Labour Party is publishing this document both as a contribution to the widespread discussion about defence as well as a demonstration of ways in which the massive defence burden can be reduced. Successive Labour Party Conferences and the 1974 Manifestos have addressed themselves to this problem and expressed concern about the high levels of defence spending, and here we present a detailed study which examines the practical consequences of taking action to reduce military expenditure.

This document presents the findings of a three-year study by a group of defence specialists who have been discussing and contributing written evidence to the National Executive Committee. We hope to publish a longer book in the near future which will contain the greater part of this evidence, and, in the meantime, the individual papers listed at the back of this text can be obtained on application from the Information Officer, The Labour Party, Transport House, Smith Square, London SW1P 3JA.

The National Executive Committee would like to record its gratitude to the members of the Study Group on Defence Expenditure, the Arms Trade and Alternative Employment, which met under the chairmanship of Mr Ian Mikardo, MP.

1

INTRODUCTION

by Ian Mikardo, MP

When the Interim Report of the Labour Party National Executive Committee's (NEC) Study Group on Defence Expenditure, the Arms Trade and Alternative Employment was published in 1976, it was seen in the press as representing a radical departure from previous policy. The truth of the matter is that Labour's interest in reducing defence spending has a long and consistent history. The discussion was brought to prominence in the early 1930s when Labour Party Conferences were already expressing concern about the waste of resources devoted to the production of arms, as well as the danger that this posed for world peace.

At the 1931 Annual Conference of the Labour Party, Hugh Dalton (later to become the Chancellor of the Exchequer) moved a resolution which read in part:

'This Conference reaffirms its belief that the present expenditure on armaments by the nations of the world is a danger to peace and to the security of the peoples, and represents a wasteful and unproductive use of a large part of the world's resources.'

The resolution was carried almost unanimously. The Labour Party's concern, however, didn't stop here. It is a tribute to the foresight of our predecessors to record that, as long ago as 1929, the Transport and General Workers' Union took the initiative in calling for the establishment of a committee to examine the economic consequences of disarmament. A tripartite committee was established in the same year, consisting of representatives from the General Council of the TUC, the National Executive of the Labour Party and delegates from the Parliamentary Labour Party. In 1931 this committee made the following recommendations:

'(a) That alternative work of suitable character not at present available to industry should be provided.
(b) That specific Government action to increase the employment in the industries chiefly affected should be taken; and in the event of neither (a) nor (b) having the desired effect –
(c) There should be adequate monetary compensation to the work people displaced.'

In 1977, after a period of some five decades, we are still facing the same problems in the defence sector; in many ways, these problems are more serious. The consumption of valuable resources by the defence industries has caused serious structural distortions in the British economy, and the very nature of modern-day warfare is more terrifying and promises even greater devastation than could have been contemplated by our predecessors.

Nevertheless, our approach to these problems remains much the same as before. In practice, this means that we seek to retain a level of defence capability appropriate to our needs, and that any cuts consequently required should not cause unemployment but be transformed into opportunities for greater economic prosperity and a more rational apportionment of the taxpayers' money. Indeed, it could even be said that the aim of our present proposals is relatively moderate. The Labour Party has translated the deeply rooted feeling that current levels of defence spending are too high and simply transformed this view into the proposal that an economically weak country like Britain should not devote a greater part of her Gross National Product to defence purposes than our European allies like Germany, France and Italy. The remit was merely to quantify the effects of the policy decided by the party and to analyse, in depth, the consequences of carrying out a reduction in defence spending of this order. This book represents the product of the NEC Defence Study Group's research and is, to the best of my knowledge, the most detailed analysis of its kind yet to have been produced.

Much of this book's emphasis relates to the economic and industrial impact of defence expenditure, and there are sound reasons for this, Nevertheless, I think that it is worth stressing

4

our very real concern about the dangers of a mounting military build-up leading to a possible Third World War. It is alarming that the tremendous skills and ingenuity of mankind have concentrated to such a great extent on the destruction of human life rather than its enrichment. While this book is being printed new weapons will be tested around the world to find better ways of killing people; today, we have a new bomb (the neutron bomb) that can kill people as a result of irreversible brain damage yet do no harm to buildings; tomorrow, another weapon might be developed which just causes some new and hideous form of physical or mental disability – and all this is done in the name of 'progress'. In 1955, when the nuclear arsenals were relatively sparse compared with today, Dr J. Robert Oppenheimer, the chief designer of the first atomic bomb, was asked on American television whether it was 'true that humans have already discovered a method of destroying humanity'. He replied : 'Not quite. You can certainly destroy enough of humanity so that only the greatest act of faith can persuade you that what is left will be human.' This, therefore, is the spectre of world war at present.

With this background in mind, I hope you will find this book worth reading and studying. What we seek to do in this book is to make a positive contribution to the wider debate about defence questions. Unfortunately, however, press comment to date has been not only misinformed, but clearly misleading. We hope that the publication of the full text of this report will provide an opportunity for a discussion on this subject based on its content rather than on emotive reactions.

BACKGROUND TO THE STUDY

The Labour Party has advocated a reduction in defence expenditure and cutbacks on the arms trade for many years. Major economic reasons for this attitude are:

1. Money spent on defence could be better used to provide public services such as housing, education and health.
2 The defence industries impede productive economic development by wasting valuable economic resources and diverting investment funds away from those industries which make socially desirable products.

This problem has been highlighted by the recent debate on public expenditure. The Labour Party cannot accept that Britain, with all her economic troubles, should go on spending a greater proportion of her Gross National Product on defence than most other Western European nations. For this reason, the 1974 General Election Manifesto promised to: 'reduce the proportion of the nation's resources devoted to defence so that the burden we bear will be brought into line with that carried by our main European allies'.

An important objection to such proposals is that they would lead to unemployment in the defence industries. We know this, and have therefore stressed methods of creating alternative employment as well as the need to use the considerable skills of workers in these industries to make a positive contribution to Britain's economic revival.

The National Executive Committee set up a study group to look into the implications of Labour's Manifesto commitment, and in particular to:

- assess the reduction in defence spending needed to meet the Manifesto commitment;
- provide a list of options of defence cutbacks which would achieve this projected reduction;
- examine the implications of these cutbacks for Britain's military and political strategy;
- calculate the impact of such cutbacks on our economic and employment situation;
- consider ways of ensuring that unemployment – even in the short term – was not a result of this policy; and
- look into possible criteria which might be used to control arms exports and examine both the impact on employment of a possible reduction in the arms trade and the opportunities for alternative employment.

The report which follows is based on a detailed, three-year study of the issues raised. The study group received evidence from a wide range of defence specialists, trade unionists from the defence industries, and politicians with an interest in this area.

The study group believes it necessary to underline the point that vast sums of taxpayers' money are spent under a cloud of quite unnecessary secrecy. No information was asked for which might be considered as undermining national security, nor would it have been thought appropriate to do so. In spite of this, in the earlier stages of the study, requests for information were frequently met by recourse of the Ministry of Defence to the claim that the disclosure of information would be prejudicial to national security, though this was not a claim that was repeated at later stages. Not only did this waste the group's time, but it illustrates that those responsible for a sector which currently consumes almost 11 per cent of the public purse are operating in an unhealthy atmosphere of distrust and secrecy which offers no guarantee that public responsibility for defence activity is not being evaded.

1

WHY CUT DEFENCE SPENDING?
A SUMMARY OF THE ARGUMENTS

> *'Just as it would be wrong to endanger national
> security in our concern for social justice, so it
> is no good having a defence policy which could
> bankrupt the society it is designed to defend.' –
> Rt Hon. Fred Mulley, MP, Secretary of State
> for Defence*[1]

Any discussions on defence spending usually
centre on the alleged dangers of reducing expenditure. Yet it is
equally valid to ask whether the real threat to our society does
not in fact come from excessively high levels of expenditure
which waste precious resources and so retard economic recovery.
At the same time it is important to recognize that any reductions
in defence spending must be accompanied by positive action to
create alternative employment for those who work in the armed
forces and defence industries. Such a programme of conversion
would demand urgent governmental action, and the departments
concerned should therefore initiate feasibility studies. And such
work should be seen as an integral part of Labour's industrial
strategy.

Although this study concentrates on the economic aspect of
defence spending, this is to be seen as a by-product rather than
the core of the subject. Defence expenditure has a clearly defined

9

purpose: it is a form of insurance which we would not need in an ideal world, but which the present state of international relations obliges us to provide. Yet it would be absurd to find that the chosen form of insurance was itself contributing to the danger it sought to avert. In other words, does not a high level of defence spending represent a threat to world security, and may not any moves to reduce this commitment lessen the tension? Meanwhile the high level of spending and the associated wastage of resources contributes to maintaining inequalities between the industrialized and non-industrialized nations – itself a further source of tension. And, as it has been argued, 'Our nuclear missiles are already killing people now, because we waste on the missiles resources which could be invested in ensuring food supplies for the world.'[2]

The arguments against maintaining the present level of defence expenditure illustrate the background to Labour's policy.

The Economic Argument

Example 1: The new Tornado (Multi-Role Combat Aircraft) project will cost about £7,000 million[3] – more than the total cost of Britain's health and personal social services for 1976/77.

Example 2: The price of the Frigate *Ambuscade* at £16 million would provide a new 508-bed hospital in Bangor.

Example 3: The submarine *Superb* is more expensive than building 4,000 new homes.

These examples indicate the magnitude of the defence burden – a burden which overall consumes 11 per cent of the nation's total public expenditure (including capital spending). More alarmingly, our defence bill accounts for nearly a quarter of the current expenditure on goods and services provided by central and local government.[4]

These facts are already fairly well known, but may hide the even greater costs of wasted resources. The defence industries employ some of our most skilled workers, consume products appropriate for capital investment and have in part been responsible for the distortion of industrial development in Britain. To state it bluntly, the defence industries have swallowed an important part of the resources so urgently needed for Britain's industrial regeneration.

Certainly Britain has an impressive record of arms production, but it has been at the expense of the socially productive side of British industry. It is often said that Britain's role in the inter-

10

national arms industry is a key factor on the positive side of our balance of payments. This is an exaggeration: at their peak, arms exports account for less than 3 per cent of total export earnings. Moreover, profits from arms exports are qualified by the need for a large home market, both to inspire confidence in the product (nobody will buy defence products from a country not prepared to use them itself) and to cover the costs of research and development. Later we will see how the export record on the military side of industries which produce both civilian and military equipment is less impressive than the sales of civilian goods. Thus considerable potential exists for both import substitution and the sale of advanced technological merchandise which could follow from a reduction in arms production.

As we have said, crucial resources and key workers are being diverted into defence production. This might not be so damaging if it could be shown that they were being sensibly used. Chapter 3 demonstrates that this is hardly the case. First, the structure of the defence industries and military bureaucracy tend to force the Government to adopt the most expensive solutions to strategic problems. Secondly, these industries are less successful in creating jobs and generating exports than their civil counterparts. This certainly suggests that some conversion of the defence sector to civil use would be more likely to improve than to damage our prospects for economic advancement.

The conversion of the defence industries is not merely an abstract proposal since the kind of changes suggested have been made elsewhere and on a much larger scale. Chapter 5 gives an industry-by-industry breakdown of conversion potential. In Britain today, much thought is being given to ways of releasing the defence industries from exclusively military production. And much of the present initiative is coming from the shop floor itself, thus giving the plans a sound basis in practical experience.

The Arms Race and the Arms Trade

The dilemma of a country like Britain, whose present economic weakness is counterpoised by a relative military strength and a capacity for high arms production, is best understood in the global context. Certain protagonists of the *status quo* argue that Britain would be foolish to abandon her share of the world arms market for an uncertain future bereft of military might. This argument is then taken further, and the existing size and importance of the defence industries is seen as a main reason for continuing to develop their potential. Arms manufacturers and

11

the government defence bureaucracy are then in a position to argue for an expansion of the military machine almost as an end in itself. This process is a continuing one, not only in Britain but in most other industrialized countries, both East and West. As others step up their arms production, so the domestic hawks see their hand strengthened as they point to increasing military power elsewhere. This is the process commonly called the 'arms race' – a race which develops an ominous momentum of its own and which can be stopped only by enlightened political action. Yet, as our studies indicate, the pressure on the defence budget from rising costs of various kinds is such as to require defence cuts simply to stand still.

The British arms industry is dependent upon arms exports. It seems rash indeed to rely on the arms industry as a major factor in Britain's economic stability, such investment being based on the inherent political instability of the customers. In other words, Britain's economic future would be dependent on recurrent wars in places like the Middle East and the continuation in power of repressive régimes. Such an attitude is not only immoral and anti-socialist but also short-sighted in both political and commercial terms.

Since Britain is a leading manufacturer of arms, she has at least a limited influence in controlling the international arms trade. In Chapter 6 this point is discussed more fully and the following proposals are made:

1. The British Government should continue to work for a multilateral arms control agreement involving both importers and exporters; while recognizing that the problems of trade are inextricably linked to the problem of production.

2. The Government should consider refusing to supply arms to states involved in international disputes, or to those régimes with a proven record of using torture and repression against their subjects.

3. A Register of Arms Sales – possibly under the auspices of the UN – should be set up. Such a central pool of information is vital if the arms trade is to be controlled.

4. Even if an international register cannot be agreed, a British register should be established.

Undoubtedly there would be considerable problems in implementing these proposals, but it could certainly be done, given the right political atmosphere.

The Political and Strategic Argument

Our high level of defence spending is a serious economic handicap. Nevertheless, Britain must have a military capacity appropriate to her defence needs. The justification of the current level of military forces is based on an official assessment of the international military balance. Our studies show, however, that the military balance is open to widely differing interpretations. Furthermore, orthodox assessments of the military balance over-emphasize technical and quantitative criteria and do not take such factors as political will or economic need sufficiently into account. It therefore seemed appropriate to examine not only the capabilities but also the intentions and interests of the USSR.

In our view, the USSR is not restrained from attacking the West by feelings of benevolence. But she is prevented from doing so by the overwhelming dangers such a step would present to the Soviet leadership itself. It is with this fact in mind that we should look at the political and strategic consequences of cutting defence spending.

Britain contributes a disproportionately high percentage of her Gross National Product (GNP) to NATO, the Western military alliance. This would be less of a problem if the United Kingdom were economically strong and the other NATO members weak. But exactly the converse is true. This imbalance is exacerbated by the steady escalation of international military tension. If Britain could cut her military spending to a level comparable to that of her European NATO allies, it would make a positive contribution to lessening international tensions and therefore actually increase international security.

Defence cuts could be carried out in various ways with varying political and strategic consequences. Three different approaches – by no means mutually exclusive or exhaustive – are discussed in Chapter 4, and are briefly:

1. A reduced British contribution to NATO might induce some of our allies to fill the gap. This would not be the aim in proposing defence cuts, but it might be the response of some of our allies with stronger economies than our own.

2. It might be possible to maintain much the same strategic capability at reduced cost by adopting more cost-effective methods, for example, by replacing expensive sophisticated weapons like Tornado with cheaper weapons which make use of the new technology of precision guidance.

13

3. We could seize the opportunity of our own defence cuts to make a contribution towards arms control.

These proposals are being made in the political climate of détente and increased effort towards mutual disarmament. Britain has the opportunity to play an active and leading part in this process. There are many reasons why we should make sure that she does.

1. *Sunday Times*, 31 October 1976.
2. Robin Cook, quoted in 'Arms Jobs and the Crisis', *CND*, July 1975.
3. See Chapter 5, under 'Alternatives in the Aerospace Industry' (p.88–9), forTornado costs; other figures from Cmnd 6735, Cmnd 6721 (vol. 11) and *Labour Research*, July 1976.
4. Figures from Government Expenditure Plans, Cmnd 6721 (11), 1977–8.

2

CURRENT DEFENCE EFFORT AND
THE NECESSARY LEVEL OF CUTS

The starting point for any programme to
reduce defence expenditure must be an examination of existing
defence effort. The following section therefore broadly sum-
marizes the current situation.

Expenditure

Despite the prevailing impression that the Government is
making great cutbacks in defence expenditure, the following
figures confirm that this is far from the case. Table 1 compares
actual defence expenditure for the first half of the 1970s, current
estimates and the Government's budgetary projections to
1980/81 on a common prices basis.

Only in the year 1977–8 has the Government managed to
bring about an actual reduction in the defence budget, and this is
only a temporary halt. Annual expenditure is expected to rise
again to over £7,000 million in the early 1980s according to
information given to the Select Committee on Expenditure.[1]

The 1977/8 figure in Table 1 is the sum actually voted in the
Defence Estimates for the current financial year. It corresponds
to about 5·5 per cent of the estimated Gross National Product
(GNP) at factor cost for 1977/8. It is envisaged that the £6,329
million will be spent as shown in Table 2. A further breakdown of
these figures is contained in Table 3, which shows the allocation
of defence expenditure to the various defence 'mission' and
'support' programmes.

Employment

The military services and industry in Britain employs, directly or indirectly, about a million people. Normally each year at least 180,000 of these can be expected to change their jobs.[2] Government figures show that the Ministry of Defence is responsible for the employment of 337,100 servicemen, and of 200,000 workers in arms industries on work projects for the Ministry, while a further 70,000 to 80,000 workers are engaged on defence exports. In addition, some 250,000 workers are indirectly employed on Ministry contracts and about 100,000 on defence exports. About 300,000 civil servants are also employed by the Ministry of Defence.[3] (See pp. 79–80 for a further regional and occupational breakdown of these figures, as well as a look in detail at some case-studies of employment in large-scale military projects.)

Military Capability[4]

The total personnel strength of the armed forces of 337,100 is relatively small in relation to the size of the British population, but conceals the leading role which Britain plays in NATO. Indeed, it is commonly accepted that Britain is the main NATO European power, largely because of Britain's naval superiority and nuclear capability. The French are also a nuclear power, but are no longer an intrinsic part of the alliance. Other indications of Britain's military strength are the large number of tanks owned by this country as well as the high degree of sophistication of the RAF. It is also widely accepted that British military personnel are of a very high standard.

Britain is also one of the few European powers to deploy numbers of troops in other parts of the world like Hong Kong and Cyprus, not to mention the 55,800 troops in the British Army of the Rhine (BAOR) in Germany. The overseas British military capability will be discussed in more detail when we come to examine the various options for cuts in the armed forces.

TABLE 1. DEFENCE EXPENDITURE, 1971–81

£ million at 1977/8 Estimates Prices

1971–2	1972–3	1973–4	1974–5	1975–6
6,638	6,460	6,395	6,164	6,448

1976–7	1977–8	1978–9	1979–80	1980–81
6,544	6,329*	6,275†	6,550†	6,550†

* Incorporates reductions in previously planned expenditure announced on 22 July and 15 December 1976.
† Provisional figure.

SOURCE: *The Government's Expenditure Plans*, vol. II, Cmnd 6721 (II), converted to 1977/8 Estimates Prices.

TABLE 2. MAJOR CATEGORIES OF EXPENDITURE, 1977/8

	£ million
Civilian pay	1,077
Equipment	2,350
Buildings and miscellaneous stores and services	1,105
Forces pay and allowances	1,452
Forces pensions	345
Total	6,329

SOURCE: *Statement on the Defence Estimates 1977*, Cmnd 6735.

The Amount of the Reduction

While Britain spends considerably more of its Gross National Product on defence than almost any other Western European nation, the share of national resources devoted to domestic investment is among the lowest in Western Europe. Britain has the largest arms industry in Europe, and it is one that is still growing. At the same time, civilian production in defence-related sectors, such as automobiles, mechanical engineering and shipbuilding, faces the most severe international competition since the war.

By how much, then, can we afford to cut defence expenditure, and how can we compare our defence burden with those of our allies? The following method is one suggestion.

The standard basis for comparing the resource cost of the defence burdens of various nations is to express the expenditure on defence as a percentage of the Gross Domestic Product (GDP). This method is not perfect, but in the words of the 1975 White Paper, 'it is the best single readily available measure of the defence burden in relation to a country's resources'.[5] The gap between Britain and her allies is, in any case, too significant to be explained by any methodological fault. In 1976, Britain's defence expenditure on the basis of the standard NATO definition was estimated at 5·2 per cent of her GDP at market prices,[6] whereas the comparable figures were 3·9 per cent for France, 3·5 per cent for Germany, and 2·6 per cent for Italy.[7] The weighted average figure for our 'main European allies' is 3·4 per cent.[8] Therefore, if it were only a question of an overnight reduction in the UK defence budget, the Manifesto commitment would imply that the budget should be brought down from 5·2 to 3·4

17

per cent of GDP: a cut of one third. However, it seems more sensible to envisage a reduction over a reasonable and specified period of time so that industrial conversion can take place more easily; the assumption here is that it would be a time period of five years.

To quantify a precise reduction in British defence expenditure to be aimed at in five years' time, we need to make two further assumptions. The first concerns the rate of real increase in the British GNP over the next five years. Between 1954 and 1973, the average annual rate of growth in the economy was 2·8 per cent. However, we start, in 1976, from a year in which there was heavy unemployment, but when we are beginning to move into a period when the balance of payments constraint on economic growth is likely to be eased by the inflow of North Sea oil. A 'central' assumption has therefore been made that, between 1976 and 1981, the average annual rate of growth in the UK economy will be 3·5 per cent a year.[9]

The second assumption concerns the likely movement, over the next five years, of the share of GDP devoted to defence among the three allies – France, Germany and Italy. The long-term trend has been for the aggregate share of their defence expenditure in GDP to fall – that is, while their military expenditure has increased, it has not increased as fast as the GDP. Thus, to avoid the objection that the calculations are based on assumptions which magnify the figure of the defence cut required in the UK, we need to assume that in all three countries military expenditure will in real terms rise significantly faster than it has done in the past. We assume that in all three countries the increase in real military expenditure is 3 per cent a year, or about double the rate of increase of the last decade. Secondly, we assume that the growth rates of GDP in the three countries from 1976–81 are fractionally lower than the long-term trend. On these two assumptions, the weighted average figure for military expenditure as a share of GDP in the three countries taken together becomes 3·2 per cent in 1981. This is more or less in line with the decisions of the May 1977 NATO Council meeting.

TABLE 3. FUNCTIONAL ANALYSIS OF DEFENCE EXPENDITURE, 1977–8
Major Programmes (and Sub-programmes)   £ *million*

MISSION PROGRAMMES

Nuclear Strategic Force – (Polaris)	96
Navy General Purpose Combat Forces	843
(a) Amphibious forces	29
(b) Aircraft carriers	15
(c) Submarines	130
(d) Cruisers	63
(e) Destroyers and frigates	319
(f) Mine counter-measures	41
(g) Other ships	116
(h) Aircraft	92
(i) Overseas shore establishments	33
(j) Fleet HQs	5
European Theatre Ground Forces	1,091
(a) BAOR	779
(b) Berlin	22
(c) Home forces	290
Other Army Combat Forces	70
(a) Hong Kong and Far East	18
(b) Mediterranean	44
(c) Other areas	8
Air Force General Purpose Forces	1,034
(a) Air defence	160
(b) Offensive support	52
(c) Strike/attack reconnaissance	280
(d) Maritime aircraft	50
(e) Transport aircraft	65
(f) Tanker aircraft	17
(g) Operational stations	148
(h) Other aircraft/civil charter/HQ/general support	262
Total mission programmes	3,134

Table 3 continued overleaf.

Reserve and Auxiliary Formation	105
Research and Development*	823
(a) Military aircraft	319
(b) Guided weapons	98
(c) Other electronics	107
(d) Naval	79
(e) Ordnance and other army	62
(f) Other R & D	158
Training	565
Production, Repair and Associated Facilities in the UK	447
(a) Naval dockyards	87
(b) Repair and maintenance	122
(c) Storage and supply	179
(d) Quality assurance	59
War and Contingency Stocks	108
Other Support Functions	1,139
Miscellaneous Expenditure and Receipts	8
Total Support Programmes	3,195
Total	6,329

* Excludes £3 million of metereological R & D included under 'Other Support Functions'.
SOURCE: 'Statement on the Defence Estimates 1977', Annex B, *Defence Data 1977/8*, Cmnd 6735.

If we bring together these central assumptions about the UK growth rate with the growth rate in Germany, France and Italy and the likely trends of military expenditure in those three countries, we can see that, to match the percentage of the national product devoted to military expenditure in the UK with that of our main European allies by 1981 (or as soon as possible thereafter), the annual military budget in this country will need to be brought down by something like *£1,825 million at 1977/8*[10] *Estimates Prices:* a cut of around 28 per cent on the expenditure projected for 1980–81 and 1981–2.

We have looked into the consequences of varying the central assumptions on which this calculation is based. What, for example, would be the consequences of a faster growth rate in the UK of 4·25 per cent a year; or of a slower growth rate of

20

2·8 per cent? What would be the consequences of a higher and lower share of national product being devoted to military expenditure in the three continental countries in 1981, taking 3·4 as the high percentage (which would mean no drop at all from the 1976 figure), and 2·8 per cent as the low point. This would be more in line with the long-term tendency for a slower rate of growth. On every combination, a substantial cut in UK military expenditure is implied: the lowest figure means a cut of some £1,250 million, the highest a cut of over £2,500 million at 1977/8 Estimates Prices. These calculations simply illustrate the size of cuts that would be needed to fulfil the Manifesto commitment; obviously they should not be seen as a rigid framework for approaching the problem. The options discussed in the following sections are, in fact, based on a rather smaller cut in military expenditure than that implied by the central assumptions set out above: on a cut of 20 per cent rather than 28 per cent.

How the Cuts Could Be Made
There are many approaches to finding ways to cut defence expenditure. This section deals with the question of looking at ways in which the defence budget *could* be reduced over the next few years if alternative judgements and assumptions were made about the nation's basic security interests, and about what constitutes 'proper provision' for defence. The options outlined are not, however, in any way prescriptive or exhaustive. The argument is based on an analysis prepared in 1975. The calculations are therefore expressed in 1975/6 Estimates Prices and designed to expose ways of attaining savings on the defence budget of £1,000 million at these prices by 1980–81, implying a reduction in the defence effort of about 20 per cent. In an updating and revaluation of the exercise undertaken just before the completion of the present report, it was concluded that the programme changes discussed might yield savings of around £1,300 million at 1977/8 Estimates Prices by 1983–4.[11] Needless to say, neither these figures nor the details of the various options should be seen as rigid formulations; both are flexible and subject to adjustment. Yet it is clear that if a cut of this order were implemented, a major reshaping of the military effort would be essential. The options outlined below have been selected from the many available choices, and a workable outcome would need the adoption of a mixture of these possibilities. Although each option has been costed, it must be emphasized that all costings are estimates based on budgeting projections; that such pro-

21

jections are in themselves tentative and subject to change. Therefore the figures given should be seen as rough guidelines in the same way that the whole exercise should be viewed as an attempt to quantify the extent of budgetary changes rather than an attempt to put forward an alternative defence programme.

Unexpected pressures on the defence budget from 'over-runs' on important equipment programmes, increased personnel costs and overall financial requirements may, in any case, force us to adopt some of the proposed modifications. It would be preferable if these could be openly anticipated and publicly discussed before they become inevitable.

Estimated Savings Possibilities on Major Programmes/ Sub-Programmes

The strategic and political consequences of adopting the selected programmes are analysed in Chapter 4. The following summary of Appendix V therefore considers only budgetary questions.The assumptions that David Greenwood has identified about current defence priorities which would be brought into question if a programme of cuts were to be implemented are as follows:

(1) A continuing commitment of ground and air forces to Allied Command Europe is crucial. But neither existing force structures nor present force levels need be regarded as sacrosanct.

(2) The Eastern Atlantic and Channel areas – including the North Sea and the Norwegian Sea – are equally vital. But the share of the Alliance effort that the United Kingdom provides might be reduced; and the nature of that provision would bear scrutiny.

(3) Ensuring the security of the 'home base' is a third co-equal priority. With the assertion of limited sovereignty over offshore areas the scope of this responsibility will grow.

(4) Neither strategic nuclear forces nor garrisons in remaining dependencies can be classed as 'essential' elements in a national order of battle constructed on the *par inter pares* basis envisaged.

This assessment leads on to the following options.

(a) Nuclear Strategic Forces

An immediate decision to withdraw Polaris submarines from service and a rundown of all associated activity. This rundown should take no more than two to three years. A plausible guess of

22

likely savings over a four-year period would be (£m at 1975–6[12] Estimates Prices):

1976–7: nil
1977–8: 50
1978–9: 50
1979–80: 75
1980–81: 75

(*b*) *Navy General Purposes Combat Forces*
Possible savings in this sphere would include:

(1) Paying off *Ark Royal*, *Hermes*, *Fearless* and *Intrepid* progressively over three to four years.
(2) Rundown of patrol submarine activity.
(3) Deletion from the programme of provision for the second and third Anti-Submarine Warfare (ASW) cruisers and, possibly, some 'stretching' of the building programme for the new destroyer and frigate classes.
(4) Reduced provision for Afloat Support (Royal Fleet Auxiliaries).
(5) Cancellation of the plans to acquire the Sea Harrier for the ASW carrier and cruisers; reduced purchases of helicopters and reduction of other costs for naval air support.

In round figures, the year-by-year distribution of these 'savings' possibilities might be as in Table 4.

TABLE 4. £m AT 1975–6 ESTIMATES PRICES

	1976–7	1977–8	1978–9	1979–80	1980–81
(1)	5	10	15	20	20*
(2)	5	10	30	40	50
(3)	–	50	100	100	150*
(4)	–	—	—	—	10*
(5)	–	10	30	40	50*
(6)†	–	—	—	—	—

[say] 275

* Denotes related sub-programmes.
† The final line is included for comparison with Table 2; no 'savings' are credited here because even a smaller ship navy would justify the retention of some overseas facilities, e.g. Gibraltar. The total is rounded to the nearest £25 million: a range 'guesstimate' would be £250–300 million.

(c) *European Theatre Ground Forces*
The whole question of troop deployments in Europe is currently under discussion and the following reductions may be envisaged:

(1) A phased rundown of the BAOR to about 30,000 by 1980/81, with appropriate adjustments in equipment purchases.
(2) No change in the Berlin garrison.
(3) Cuts in Home Forces to reflect the reduced roulement requirement of a smaller Rhine Army.

The order of magnitude of budgetary 'savings' attainable on this programme would be as in Table 5.

TABLE 5. £m AT 1975–6 ESTIMATES PRICES

	1976–7	1977–8	1978–9	1979–80	1980–81
(1)	—	50	100	150	200*
(2)	—	—	—	—	—
(3)	—	—	25	50	75*
					275

* Denotes related items. 'Savings' possibilities under (1) would be lower if, as a counterpart to 'savings' on RAF Germany, it were decided that the Rhine Army should have enhanced missile air defences and/or improved artillery capabilities.

(d) *Other Army Combat Forces*
Relatively minor savings are foreseen for the reduction of army strengths outside Europe; they would, however, contribute to an existing rundown of forces in this sphere. A phased reduction or gradual increase in contributions towards maintaining these overseas troops might yield 'savings' in the intervening years as follows (£m at 1975–6 Estimates Prices):

1976–7: nil
1977–8: 5
1978–9: 10
1979–80: 20
1980–81: 25

(e) *Air Force General Purposes Forces*
Savings in the Royal Air Force would demand the reshaping of

the force to concentrate on the effective performance of a more limited range of roles in place of the present broader spectrum of mission capabilities. Possibilities for 'savings' might then include the following:

(1) Deletion from the programme of provision for the air defence variant (ADV) of the Multi-role Combat Aircraft (MRCA) Tornado. Phantoms would have to fulfil the air defence task throughout the 1980s if the Tornado interceptor were cancelled. Improvements in them and their Sparrow missiles would therefore be necessary. Increased provision of surface-to-air missiles (SAMs) is another possibility for reinforcing the army's ability to defend itself from air attack. Savings on the cancelled Tornado programme would therefore need to be assessed alongside these considerations.
(2) Additional expenditure on Jaguar, and perhaps on Harrier, would also need to be set against Tornado savings. These aircraft have a strike/attack capacity, but may not be as cost-effective as a plane like the Fairchild A10. So here is another possibility for replacement.
(3) Arising from a reassessment of mission priorities and the creation of a 'lower cost air force', a substantial reduction in strike/attack/reconnaissance could be envisaged by cancellation of the 'common' strike/reconnaissance Tornado version.
(4) Such a reassessment would also allow for reductions in the support programme; namely, reduced provision for tanker aircraft and transport squadrons.
(5) Further closures of operational stations, or reduced running costs of existing ones.
(6) Some reduction in the expense of general support and headquarters. These are largely administrative costs.

Table 6 gives a broad estimate for a plausible scenario for 'savings', these figures being subject to wider margins of error than those used previously. This is because the net 'savings' illustrated would be applicable only in the immediate future owing to the effect of cancellation charges and because much of this speculation relates to the provision of substitutes where the problem of costing is complex. Nevertheless, this is what the position in round figures might be.

Table 6. £m at 1975–6 Estimates Prices

	1976–7	1977–8	1978–9	1979–80	1980–81
(1) ⎫					
(2) ⎬	—	—	180	200	220*
(3) ⎭					
(4)	—	—	—	5	10
(5)	—	—	5	10	15
(6)	5	10	15	20	30*
					275

* Denotes related sub-programmes. The attribution of early 'savings' to (6) presupposes immediate decisions on Tornado to permit 'support' economies; that of a minor and late 'saving' to (4) is explained by the fact that further transport squadron cuts would not be possible until the end of the period, and could not even then be extensive.

(f–l) Support Programmes
A further 'savings' potential with regard to shifts in defence programme options of this size lies in the reduction of support programmes. At present there is a ratio of 54:46 per cent between expenditure on mission and support programmes. It would therefore be reasonable to expect support function to yield at least a third of possible savings. The cumulative effect of this would be to produce a 'saving' of something like £325–350 million in the period to 1980/81. The source of these savings could therefore be as listed in Table 7.

Table 7. Support Programme
£m at 1975–6 Estimates Prices

(f) Reserve forces	15
(g) R & D not included elsewhere	50
(h) Training	75
(i) Production, repair and associated facilities	50
(j) Other support functions (miscellaneous heading for Whitehall organization, local administration, personal pensions and services for armed forces, etc.)	125
(k–l) Stocks/miscellaneous expenditure and receipts	35
	350

Defence Programme Options to 1980–81
Having identified areas where savings could be made, we now

need to suggest various ways in which these savings could be combined throughout the services to achieve the target level of cuts. Implicit in this exercise is the attempt to achieve a balance which will ensure that essential defence needs are met. This means that, while the exercise allows for a relaxation of assumptions on the right level of provision, it is also involved in a more stringent definition of security priorities.

By showing the scope for possible 'savings', three leading options have emerged as providing likely arrangements for a reduced defence effort. In this scenario, the rundown of the Polaris force and facilities, and the dropping from the current planned programme of expenditure on army combat forces outside Europe, are common to all three option programmes. Cuts in two of the three remaining mission programmes (b, c, or e), would also need to be implemented. And finally, it would be necessary to make appropriate cuts in support programmes if a reduction of around one sixth of present planned expenditure is to be achieved by 1980–81.

A fourth option would be to retain the Polaris programme and make larger cuts in other areas; or a further possibility is to tackle the question by attempting a mix of options within the various sub-headings of the major mission programmes.

On this basis, the following options emerge:

(1) Adopt the smaller ship fleet philosophy and make reductions in European Theatre Ground Forces (ETGF) while planning to maintain a 'full spectrum' Royal Air Force, complete (in time) with nearly 400 Tornados. *Or*
(2) elect to move to both a smaller ship fleet *and* a lower-cost air force, thus avoiding the necessity for reducing ETGF levels. *Or*
(3) preserve the existing naval programme, with its balanced fleet philosophy ('ships of high quality'), allowing the burden of adjustment to fall on the Royal Air Force, notably RAF Germany, and on the BAOR and the UK land forces.

Options 1 and 2 would be 'available', so to speak, with or without a somewhat diminished submarine force; Options 2 and 3 with a larger or smaller complement of maritime, transport and tanker aircraft.

The fourth option, which envisages the retention of Polaris, would involve further reductions in all three major conventional force programmes. In the naval sector, this could mean stretching

27

the fleet submarine, destroyer and frigate building programmes. In the European theatre, it implies a marginally sharper rundown of men to around 27,500 with an appropriate adjustment in support functions and home forces. And it is assumed that the necessary air-force cuts will come from the Tornado and related programmes sector.

There are at least four other implicit options: those which follow from the remaining permutations possible on the 'heavy-weight' service programmes. They do not, however, hit the 1980–81 budget target: one of them would yield greater 'savings', the rest a good deal less. But they are none the less worth stating, giving, as they do, a general indication of the broader range of choice.

In principle, if all the 'rationales for options' were thought especially compelling, it would be possible to:

(5) Opt for the smaller ship fleet *and* reduced ETGF levels *and* a lower cost air force – entailing an all-round diminution of military stature.

But if, on the other hand, reconsideration of priorities and 'proper provision' were thought possible for only one service's roles, the options would be:

(6) The smaller ship fleet. *Or*
(7) the reduced ETGF levels. *Or*
(8) the lower cost air force.

In summary, the 'guesstimates' for costings of the options discussed would be as in Table 8.

TABLE 8. PROGRAMME OPTIONS TO 1980–81: OPTIONS FOR
DEFENCE BUDGET TARGET (Target 'Savings': £1,000m at
1975–6 Estimates Prices. These figures would be around
£1,800m in 1977–8 Estimates Prices)

Defence Budget Saving 1980–81 (£m)

Option 1
(*a*) Rundown Polaris and facilities	75	
(*b*) Smaller ship fleet	275	(225)
(*c*) Reduced ETGF levels	275	
(*d*) No cost to UK arrangements	25	
	——	
Mission programmes	650	
(*f-l*) Proportionate reductions	*c.* 350	
	—— *c.* 1,000 (925)	

28

Option 2

(a) Rundown Polaris and facilities	75	(225)
(b) Smaller ship fleet	275	(225)
(d) No cost to UK arrangements	25	
(e) Lower cost air force	275	(265)
	——	
Mission programmes	650	
(f-l) Proportionate reductions	c. 350	
	——	c. 1,000 (900)

Option 3

(a) Rundown Polaris and facilities	75	
(c) Reduced ETGF levels	275	
(d) No cost to UK arrangements	25	
(e) Lower cost air force	275	(265)
	——	
Mission programmes	650	
(f-l) Proportionate reductions	c. 350	
	——	c. 1,000 (985)

Note: Figures in parentheses identify the effects of excluding 'non-related' items, i.e. submarine reductions in (b) and tankers and other aircraft reductions in (e).

Option 4 would demand greater reductions in two or more of the main mission programmes, plus the necessary proportionate reductions in support programme outlays to 'compensate' for retention of the Polaris force. The composition of savings attainable for Options 5–8 can be inferred from the information for Options 1–3.[13]

As explained at the outset, this detailed analysis was originally undertaken in 1975. It is clear, however, that the possibilities outlined as programme change options remain more or less valid today. The savings they would allow could, however, hardly be attained by 1980–81. Moreover, the value of the eventual reduction in the defence budget which they would make possible needs to be translated into 1977–8 Estimates Prices for comparison with the current and planned future defence expenditure levels set out in Tables 1–3. In fact, the transposition in timing is not at all troublesome if it is assumed (a) that not even early decisions on a reshaping of the defence effort could begin to yield significant savings before 1979/80, but that (b) the savings allotted in the above paragraphs to 1977/8 to 1980/81 would be attainable in the period 1979/80 to 1983/4, subject only to minor modification

29

(to reflect, for instance, increased cancellation costs on projects now further advanced).

Conversion of the projected savings to 1977/8 Estimates Prices is similarly straightforward. The most succinct statement of the essential argument of this chapter is therefore the presentation in Table 9. It shows the budgetary projections for the current defence programme (from Table 1), and the time profiles of expenditure which would be associated with the three principal options discussed above (pp. 27–9), on the retiming and revaluation assumptions just stated.

TABLE 9. PROGRAMME OPTIONS TO 1983–4 (£m at 1977–8 Estimates/1977 Survey Prices)

Programme	1979–80	1980–81	1981–2	1982–3	1983–4
Current					
(From Table 1)	6,550	6,550	6,550	(6,900)	(7,200)
Option 1	6,543	6,250	6,000	6,000	5,900
'Savings'	7	300	550	900	1,300
Option 2	6,535	6,325	5,900	5,900	5,900
'Savings'	15	225	650	1,000	1,300
Option 3	6,550	6,400	6,000	5,900	5,900
'Savings'	—	150	550	1,000	1,300

SOURCE: See Appendix V to full report, Postscript.

Conclusion

The courses of action reviewed would allow an estimated reduction of around £1,300 million in the defence budget by 1983/4 – a 20 per cent reduction measured against the forecast expenditure level of the late 1970s. It must be re-emphasized that this exercise is not prescriptive; it does not provide a blueprint for a new defence strategy in the 1980s. The intention has been to give an impression of the kind of changes needed to achieve a re-shaping of the armed forces if savings of this kind are to be achieved.

Notes and References
1. See Second Report from the Expenditure Committee, Session 1976–7, HC 254 (76/77), Report, p. x.
2. Appendix XII: F. Blackaby, 'Note on the Employment Consequences of a £1,000m. Cut (at 1974 Prices) in Military Expenditure Over 5 years'.
3. *Hansard*, col. 42, 9 October 1976; and Cmnd 6735.
4. Information for this section from Cmnd 6735 and *The Military Balance 1976–1977*, IISS, 1977.

5. 'Statement on the Defence Estimates 1975', Cmnd 5976.
6. This estimate is taken from *Economic Trends*, April 1977, adjusted to the standard UN definition. The definition of GDP at market prices is approximately 3·5 per cent below the figure given in UK national accounts.
7. Estimate calculated from *UN Monthly Bulletin of Statistics*, March 1977. This is an estimate NIESR based on known movements in outputs and price changes.
8. The weights are derived from the estimates of GDP to US dollars in *UN Monthly Bulletin of Statistics*, March 1977.
9. 'World Armaments and Disarmament', *SIPRI Year Book*, 1974 p. 133.
10. 1977/8 Estimates Prices are the basis on which the government is planning its current expenditure programmes; these figures represent actual price levels in September 1976.
11. The material which follows is based on studies prepared for the NEC by David Greenwood: *Defence Programme Options to 1980–81* (the original analysis, completed September 1975); and a postscript to that paper (written May 1977). Both appear at Appendix V in the full report.
12. These are the figures from the original analysis; for revised assessments, attributed to the period to 1983–4, see the Postscript in ibid.
13. For details, see Appendix VI in the full report.

3

DEFENCE EXPENDITURE AND
THE ECONOMY

Decisions about the level and nature of defence spending are not only political. They are also decisions about the social allocation of resources, about how to decide between competing claims on public expenditure and how to reconcile strategic requirements, as seen by defence planners, with economic and social needs. There seems, in fact, to be a lack of evidence for the notion that higher levels of defence spending or the maintenance of current levels bring economic advantages. Instead we have drawn two somewhat contrary and disturbing conclusions: first, that governments have tended to adopt the most expensive solutions to strategic problems, often in contradiction to declared policy objectives – which can be explained only in terms of the structure of the institutions responsible for the research, development, production and operation of military equipment; secondly, that these same expensive solutions have had harmful effects on the civilian economy. Defence spending actually affects the economy at a number of 'sore points':

1. It requires a relatively high skill-content, both in the production of weapons and in their operation; and a perennial problem of the British economy has been the shortage of skilled workers.
2. It absorbs a very high proportion of the research and development effort of the United Kingdom.

33

3. Because consumption and welfare spending represent a relatively stable proportion of national income, military spending is, in expenditure terms, directly competitive with investment.

4. It has a specifically heavy impact on the engineering sector of the economy, which is the sector also responsible for a relatively high proportion of our exports and investment goods.

5. Particularly because of the cost of maintaining troops in Germany, there is a high balance of payments cost; and again, the balance of payments has been one of the perennial weaknesses of the British economy.

6. Finally, the whole of defence expenditure falls in the public expenditure category; and it is widely held that the levels of taxation, particularly on the average wage-earner, associated with the present level of public expenditure are damagingly high.

All these factors suggest that the restructuring and redeployment of Britain's defence industry is an essential condition both for cutting defence expenditure and finding cheaper solutions to strategic problems, as well as for regenerating the British economy. The present chapter provides the background to these issues. Chapter 5 will detail specific proposals for conversion and diversification opportunities.

Defence Decision-making and the Economy: Choice of Projects
A major cause for concern is the cost of particular weapon programmes which have come to dominate the British defence budget. Current examples are the Multi-Role Combat Aircraft (Tornado) and the ASW Cruiser. The Expenditure Committee of the House of Commons recently concluded that:

> The Ministry (MOD) have occasionally appeared to aim for so high a standard that either projects have had to be abandoned or sacrifices have had to be made elsewhere in the defence programme in order to limit or accommodate escalating costs.[1]

The increase in the cost of new generations of military equipment has been remarkable. For example, it has been calculated[2] that the real cost of producing 385 Tornados will be slightly greater than the entire production costs of Spitfire before and during the Second World War. Taking account of inflation and other cost increases, it was shown that the cost per ton of warships has increased by anything from a factor of 10 (the difference between an early post-war 'Bay' class frigate and the last of a long series of 'Leander' class frigates) to a factor of 15 (the difference between an early post-war 'A' class submarine and a modern 'Swiftsure' class submarine, or between the Vanguard Battleship and the new Anti-Submarine Warfare Cruiser).

If anything, these figures are understated since they refer only to production costs. Total life-cycle costs would be even more striking, since maintenance and support costs tend to increase faster than production costs because of the unreliability of highly complex and sophisticated equipment. In particular, there is the increase in electronic equipment, which accounts for much of the overall cost: a rise in requirements here involves a disproportionate increase in what are called logistic support costs.

Increases in cost are thus related to increases in the sophistication and complexity of military equipment designed to meet more stringent and elaborate performance targets. Obvious recent examples are the variable geometry aircraft (i.e. the swing-wing) designed to increase flexibility and multiply an aircraft's possible functions; gas-turbine engines for surface warships, designed to increase speed; nuclear propulsion for submarines, to increase their speed and range; and the various types of electronic equipment which are to be found across the whole range of weapons systems and which vastly improve communications, navigation, the identification and detection of enemy targets and the guidance of weapons, and which can reduce the effectiveness of enemy electronic equipment. These are the major technological changes. There are also continual developments in existing technologies – increases in the thrust of a given type of jet engine, improvements in the accuracy of a particular kind of guidance system. Over time, marginal developments of this kind have tended to involve a disproportionate increase in costs.

Technical advance can always be explained in strategic terms. In peacetime, however, the assessment of any threat is necessarily subjective. Changes in technology, by inducing new perceptions and counter-perceptions of the threat, can propel planners into further changes in an autistic fashion. The idea of defence as a race against technology originated during the Second World War, and it has come to have an existence apparently independent of changes in the political and economic environment. Representatives of the arms sector tend to view technology as an end in itself, and regret cancelled projects simply because they represent a loss of technical leadership. One well-established writer, for example, explains that because the Ministry of Defence were sceptical of the variable geometry aircraft concept 'on the grounds of both time and price', and were unwilling to finance continued research by Vickers during the 1950s, it 'became imperative that some manned military application be found for all the theories and tests'.[3] This was the origin of Tornado. And yet, as we shall see in Chapter 4, it is questionable whether increased sophistication really represents technical advance and improvement, whether, in fact, it genuinely represents the optimum approach to strategic problems. Several defence critics are concerned about the unreliability, vulnerability and lack of manoeuvrability of modern weapons systems. The fact that such doubts exist, and have even manifested themselves in thwarted attempts to control costs by cancelling major projects, suggests that the problem lies less with hardware and strategic perceptions and more with the underlying military-industrial structure.

This is not to say that the underlying structure of the defence industries is the sole influence on decisions about military procurement, but it does remain the major consideration. Other significant influences have also been suggested. J. R. Kurth, examining the factors influencing a particular procurement decision in the USA, identified four main types of consideration that could be important: (i) strategic or geo-political considerations, (ii) bureaucratic self-interest and inertia within the compartmentalized defence hierarchy; (iii) electoral calculations by politicians (vide the increase in the 'Soviet menace' shortly after Mrs Thatcher assumed the Tory leadership); and (iv) the needs and interests of the defence contractors.[4] There is every indication that the same considerations are the main determinants of procurement in Britain.

The Structure of the Defence Industry

The capacity to develop and produce military hardware may in general terms be defined as the amount of plant, machinery and labour available for development and production over a given time period. It may be measured, in abstract monetary terms, as maximum output in the given period. In specific terms, however, it represents an infrastructure of skills and techniques, and a set of relationships between the services and the sub-contractors needed to manufacture a particular type of military equipment.

With the nationalizing of the shipbuilding and aerospace industries, much of the defence industry is now under public control. It is to be hoped that the newly nationalized companies will not operate according to the principles of private enterprise, which necessarily mean the principle of independent viability, and hence of profit making. In the past, this has meant that individual defence companies were responsible for financing manufacturing capacity and could not afford long periods of idleness. In a centrally planned economy, where private criteria of efficiency are not the sole determinant, alternative uses can be found for industrial capacity in the pauses between military orders. In the USSR, for example, buffer production has been a central feature of the armaments industry since 1955.[5]

But with the increase in the sophistication of military equipment, military technology has become increasingly divorced from civilian technology, and consequently industrial capacity has become increasingly specialized. The Government is meanwhile the main customer for military equipment in such a way as to avoid excess capacity. As Vice-Admiral Clayton explains:

> We have to give the shipbuilders a regular rolling programme of orders. We depend on the specialist warshipbuilders. They have a very carefully balanced selection of trades – drawing office, steel workers and outfit trades – which are required especially for warshipbuilding and not for commercial shipbuilding, and of necessity we have to keep a flow of orders going to them.[6]

Avoiding surplus capacity is not simply a matter of employment, but also involves expansion. The principle of independent viability entails the principle of profit maximization and the constant striving after technical change. In a competitive situation – competition being defined in its broadest sense – firms must innovate, they must introduce new ideas, designs and products, if they are to maintain their markets. This applies as much in the military as the civilian sphere: firms must keep up with wider international developments in military technology if they are to continue to receive orders and if the armed services are, in turn, to justify those orders. In this way, of course, they contribute to the strategic developments they are trying to match.

Yet new technological developments must be paid for, and that means an increase in orders and hence an expansion of capacity.*

* It might be objected that companies could compete through process innovation, through developing cheaper solutions to military problems. The problem is that such developments might undermine the existing market, leading the Government to reduce military spending and abandon the current inventory of sophisticated equipment as well as removing the *raison d'être* of the specialized defence firm.

The striving for technical progress becomes the more extreme the more limited the market. We have seen how the cost of competition has risen in recent years in the automobile and merchant shipbuilding industry. The same is true of defence. The more the Government has reduced the numbers of types of weapons, the greater has been the effort to achieve technical progress and the greater the compensating cost increase.

In the last fifteen years, Hawker Siddeley has produced or developed seven military aircraft, including two that were cancelled; and BAC has developed or produced six military aircraft, including two that were cancelled. In the previous fifteen years, the companies that amalgamated to form Hawker Siddeley and BAC developed or produced twenty-eight and eighteen military aircraft respectively, as well as several other research aircraft. The number of aircraft produced of any given type has likewise declined substantially, yet the increase in the cost of each individual aircraft is such as to compensate for the decline in numbers. The same phenomenon is to be found in shipbuilding. In the period 1965–74, about half as much warship tonnage was launched as during the period 1945–54. Yet real costs have increased by factors ranging from 10 to 15, leading to a substantial overall increase in warship-building capacity.[7]

The explanation of this trend need not be seen simply in crude capitalistic terms. It is also a matter of redeployment following numerical reductions in orders. Designers shifted from one project to another, bringing with them pet ideas that could always find supporters within the services. The alternative to a rigorous elimination of unnecessary ideas and choosing between competing ideas is the compromise of doing everything.

Attempted Solutions
Governments of all arms-producing countries whose defence sectors play a major economic role are well aware of the problems inherent in the existence of surplus capacity in the defence industries. Current attempts to rectify the problem identify three possible solutions: first, to cultivate expanding export markets; secondly, to reorganize the defence industry; and thirdly, to set up international collaboration in the development and production of military equipment. It may be said with reasonable confidence that none of these solutions has worked in the past or is likely to work in the future.

Export orders account for between 20 and 30 per cent of British arms production. Since this proportion is relatively stable and tends to change primarily in response to world demand, exports can rarely provide a substitute for increased government orders. Neither do exports cover the costs of maintaining development capacity. The Ministry of Defence has had considerable difficulty in recent years in recovering the levy on the sale of military equipment developed at government expense. Moreover, only about a third of the Ministry's sales of military equipment in the financial year 1975–6 achieved a 'target price of full economic cost including all overhead expenses and return on capital'.[8] (There are also political and strategic problems attached to a dependence on the export trade; these and a fuller examination of the economic aspects will be considered in Chapter 6.)

The second solution, the reorganization of the defence industry, has had only a limited success. This is because amalgamation has not involved rationalization. Attempts to reduce the number of defence firms and the number of weapons systems have led to increased complexity and inefficiency as a result of cooperation between competing plants, and hence to increased cost and industrial capacity. Such attempts include the 1957 'Suicide' White Paper (which advocated the replacement of manned aircraft by missiles), the failure of the first of the great multi-role aircraft, the TSR-2[9] (itself a fitting prelude to the even more costly Tornado), and the decision to phase out aircraft carriers in 1966 (which was followed by a costly generation of destroyers, frigates and anti-submarine warfare cruisers). With the progressive reduction in the number of types of weapon delivery systems, the process of further rationalization will eventually reach a logical limit, at least on a national basis.

International collaboration in the manufacture of weapons, on the other hand, reproduces the problem of excess capacity on a grander international scale. So long as individual nations continue to protect their military manufacturing capacity, international collaboration must remain little more than a cooperative form of duplication. From the point of view of industry, international projects have the great advantage that they are less liable to be cancelled. From the point of view of the public, international collaboration means even less parliamentary control, and even greater cost escalation. The difficulties of amalgamating the design teams of two separate companies and reconciling a number of service requirements at a national level pale into insignificance when compared with the difficulty of amalgamating design teams from several different countries and of reconciling the requirements of distinctly separate national armed forces. Hence the dramatic cost increases in Jaguar, the Anglo-French helicopters and, above all, Tornado (not to mention Concorde). When the Anglo-French variable geometry aircraft was cancelled, General Gallois, French Director of Military Affairs, told *The Times* that, on a co-operative project, 'you divided the cost by two and then had to multiply it by three to take account of the difficulties of building it in two countries'.[10]

The Economic Effects of Defence Decisions

Apologists for military spending suggest that the problem of resource allocation is magnified. They argue that defence production yields economic benefits in the form of technological spin-off, employment and exports. The conclusions of the present study, however, suggest that this argument is fallacious. Military spending tends to be inversely correlated with industrial investment, and hence with economic growth. There is a good deal of evidence to show that the expenditure of a given amount of resources in the military sector tends to generate less employment and exports than an equivalent deployment of resources in the civil sector of the same industries. And the advantages of spin-off are likely to be offset by the disadvantages of 'militarizing' science and technology.

Nevertheless, in the short term, a direct transfer of resources would not necessarily rectify the problem. This is especially true in a period when the economy is stagnant and transitional problems could be considerable.

When evaluating any given defence programme, the money totals are often a misleading indication of the true economic costs. For instance, it might be cheaper in terms of direct expenditure to run a conscript army, but in conditions of full employment it would be wasteful of resources to tie up a sizeable proportion of the labour force solely on grounds of cutting direct spending. It is therefore necessary also to consider the opportunity and resource costs of the expenditure. David Greenwood defines the former as being a 'reminder that spending entails allocation and choice among competing opportunities'.[11] The concept of opportunity cost therefore raises the question of priorities, but it is necessary in addition to consider the extent to which the resources available can actually be substituted or transferred between competing programmes or uses in the short term. This will depend on a variety of factors, such as whether the workers and equipment which the project would use are currently being employed at all. If they are unemployed, the resource cost may be very small. And apart from how specific the available factors of production may be, alternative options for (in this case) public expenditure must take into account whether, for example, it would be better to raise the school leaving age than continue with the Tornado project.

An assessment of resource cost involves a choice between real substitutes. The factors of production used for the Tornado programme, for example, are quite specific: skilled labour, R & D facilities, specialized machine tools and so forth. They could not provide the classrooms, teachers and educational materials needed to raise the school leaving age in the short run. On the other hand, the same resources might be in short supply elsewhere in the economy, in the machine-tool sector, for instance, and the resulting short-term bottlenecks could have long-term consequences, through loss of markets or technical leadership among other factors. The absorption of specific kinds of resource needs elsewhere in the civilian economy may be called resource cost.

Ron Smith has identified five major factors which determine resource cost:[12]

(1) The degree of utilization in the various sectors.
(2) The multiplier and linkage effects between sectors.
(3) The degree of substitution possible between commodities, both in the pattern of production and the pattern of expenditure.
(4) The costs involved in adjusting from one pattern of input and output competition to another.
(5) The rates of growth in the different sectors.

Taken together, these factors show the availability of resources; the cumulative effect of changes in use; the degree of specificity in production and the area of choice available in the light of social and political priorities; the costs of conversion; and the fact that growth brings an increase in flexibility.

In perspective, therefore, the major distinction is not really between 'opportunity cost' and 'resource cost', but rather between the resources which could be transferred in the short term, and those which could be transferred in the long term. We now examine the different kinds of resources.

41

(a) Labour

The Labour movement's concern is tackling the problem of defence expenditure is to ensure that reductions do not involve any rise in unemployment. The fact is, however, that defence has a lower immediate impact on domestic employment than any other form of government expenditure. This is because defence production is more capital-intensive than other kinds of production. Three per cent of the economically active population in Britain, some 625,000 people,[13] is employed by the military sector.

International comparisons show how countries with high shares of military expenditure also tend to have higher than average unemployment rates. Britain and the United States, in particular, show this characteristic, while Japan and Germany have lower rates of unemployment coupled with lower shares of military expenditure. This is partly explained by reasons already outlined, but is also because the pernicious effect of defence expenditure on investment, productivity, growth and the balance of payments has meant that states with high levels of military expenditure have had to deflate the economy more, and so create more unemployment in attempts to get their balances of payments into equilibrium.

The Labour Party's programme of defence spending cuts would create the need for new jobs; a detailed examination of how this would be done is contained in Chapter 5. The basic point is that a greater long-term potential for creating more jobs with secure employment leads more from reducing the military budget than from maintaining a large military budget in a weak economy. There are considerable problems in shifting the allocation of public expenditure from one place to another, and the short-term effects of such a reallocation could only be beneficial if stringent planning procedures were adopted.

(b) Investment

It has been seen how investment and military spending are directly competitive, and how a high level of defence spending is therefore likely to produce a low level of industrial investment, a factor which in turn inhibits economic growth.

Military spending is competitive with investment in two senses. First, it is competitive with investment in expenditure terms. In advanced industrialized countries, the share of national income devoted to consumption is fairly stable. Therefore investment tends to compete with public expenditure, notably with

42

military expenditure. This holds true for the British historical experience as well as in cross-country comparisons. Since the war, investment in Britain has tended to rise when military spending has fallen and vice versa.[14] Table 10 shows the share of GNP devoted to military spending and investment in advanced industrial countries. It shows that the highest military spenders, the United States and Britain, are the lowest domestic investors, and that the highest domestic investor, Japan, is the lowest military spender. Military spending is also competitive with investment in resource terms since arms are produced in the same industries as capital goods. Whereas military spending accounted for only about 5 per cent of GNP, domestic military purchases represented, in 1971, about 7 per cent of mechanical engineering output, nearly 30 per cent of electronics and telecommunications output, over half of shipbuilding output, and three quarters of aerospace output.

A key determinant of economic growth is engineering output. In the 1950s, Germany and Japan were able to devote a greater proportion of engineering output to investment and exports than we were. In approximate terms, it has been estimated that in the UK it needs an additional £1·00 of investment to produce an additional £0·30 of output.[15] It is therefore reasonable to assume that if this investment were taken away from the military sector and put into the civil sector, it would create increased output, jobs and exports. And this assumes merely a constant level of productivity. It does not take into account the increases in productivity that might be expected from increased investment. Nor does it take into account the effect on prices. Such inflation is fuelled by the failure of productivity to keep up with wage increases, but a faster rate of productivity would slow inflation and thus would increase exports, output and real wages. Hence military spending, when compared with other factors, represents a *loss* of jobs, exports, income, productivity, growth and lower prices.

43

TABLE 10. INVESTMENT AND MILITARY EXPENDITURE: OECD COUNTRIES, 1974

Country	Military expenditure* (US $ × 10⁶)	Military expenditure as percentage of GNP* %	Investment as percentage of GDP† %	Average annual growth-rate in GNP 1963–73‡ %
United States	85,900	6·15	18	3·9
United Kingdom	10,000	5·24	20	2·7
France	10,600	3·63	25	5·7
West Germany	13,800	3·58	22	4·7
Netherlands	2,320	3·45	22	5·4
Sweden	1,780	3·10	22	3·4
Norway	671	3·13	32	4·7
Italy	4,630	2·93	23	4·8
Belgium	1,460	2·77	22	4·8
Denmark	728	2·37	22	4·5
Canada	2,790	2·05	23	5·2
Switzerland	856	1·91	27	4·0
New Zealand	237	1·75	26	3·4
Finland	255	1·31	29	4·9
Austria	292	0·91	28	5·2
Luxembourg	18	0·87	26	3·4
Japan	3,670	0·83	34	10·5

* US Arms Control and Disarmament Agency, 1976 (Washington DC: US Government Printing Office, 1976): *World Military Expenditures and Arms Transfers 1965–74*.
† United Nations Department of Economic and Social Affairs Statistical Office, *Statistical Yearbook, 1975* (New York: United Nations, 1976).
‡ US Arms Control and Disarmament Agency, 1974 (Washington DC: US Government Printing Office): *World Military Expenditures and Arms Transfers 1963–73*

(c) *Research and Development*

Research and development (R & D) activity could be described as 'future investment' because the amount of attention paid to this aspect can have a crucial impact on the development of the economy. Military spending absorbs investible resources, and, in particular, some of the most valuable of these resources – the trained engineers and scientists who contribute directly to technical progress and competitiveness. The success of the

44

German machine-tool industry, for example, is not just a result of greater manufacturing capacity, it is also due to the German ability to innovate – to design the package machine-tool, for example. British R & D expenditure is more biased towards the military than that of almost any other Western industrial nation. The true implications of this cannot be gleaned from the figures given. Technical progress foregone is not measurable. Furthermore, it is not just a matter of diverting resources from military to civil purposes. The prevalence of military work has imposed a certain mentality on engineers and scientists – a preoccupation with sophistication and emphasis on complex and elaborate pieces of equipment instead of the cheap and simple products which people can actually use. Even in the civil field, much British R & D effort has gone into nuclear energy and Concorde. One important reason for the failure of British merchant ship-building since 1945 has been the cost of sophisticated facilities designed for naval use. In addition, this mentality has reduced the supposed benefits from spin-off. The increasing sophistication of military hardware in general has actually lessened the possibility of applying such technology in the civil sphere.[16]

The situation seen on a sector-by-sector basis shows an even more alarming picture of the uneven deployment of resources. Almost half the total government-sponsored R & D is devoted to defence.[17] In cash terms, the 1977/8 allocation for military R & D is £826 million, while the total agricultural R & D allocation for 1976 was £34 million and the Medical Research Council will be receiving only £27·5 million.[18] Sixty per cent of qualified scientists and engineers in the mechanical engineering industry work on arms, which represent less than 7 per cent of output. Similarly, while half of shipbuilding output is purchased by the navy, 90 per cent of R & D expenditure in shipbuilding is devoted to naval work.

In the discussion of occupational conversion later in this study (pp. 87–8), we will also consider the effect of the whole ethos prevailing in the arms industries which produces attitudes that are incompatible with the aims of an efficient civil sector. Unless an effort is made to redress the balance between research and development in the civil and military sectors, no amount of new capital will produce the kind of real boost needed to regenerate British industry.

(d) *Exports*

Chapter 6 is devoted to the arms trade, and so takes an overall look at the implications of this trade; the purpose of this brief section is therefore primarily to show how, contrary to much current propaganda, the export of arms is not the most efficient aspect of our overseas trade. The defence-related industries are the most export-intensive industries, i.e. machinery and transportation. In 1971, the total military and non-military exports of the defence-related industries was 40 per cent of total output.[19] This is probably a representative figure as 1971 does not seem to be an exceptional year. In contrast to this figure, arms exports as a percentage of total arms production (domestic procurement plus exports) is about 25 per cent. In other words, the very same resources – machinery, plant and people – when devoted to defence produce fewer exports than when they are devoted to civilian production. This difference has probably increased in recent years since exports of machinery and transportation have increased faster than output as a whole, while the ratio of military exports to military production has changed little.

Professor Kurt Rothschild has applied these facts to the various theories of export-led economic growth (currently popular in Treasury circles). He argues that high levels of military expenditure reduce export opportunities, which in turn slows down growth in GNP.[20] This hypothesis is difficult to prove conclusively, but it is worthy of consideration even if all it eventually shows is that export performance could hardly be any worse with a reduced arms sector, and is likely to be much better.

(e) *Defence and the Balance of Payments*
Another rarely observed aspect of the impact of military spending and its relation to the economy is the net loss suffered by the balance of payments as a result of stationing troops in Germany and elsewhere, and from importing American military aircraft. Table 11 presents the figures given in the Statement on Defence Estimates of the balance of payments effects of military expenditure.

46

TABLE 11.

	1976–7 £m	1977–8 £m
Cost of stationing troops abroad	690	696
Other military services*	160	147
Purchases of military equipment	167	258
Total debits	1,017	1,101
Receipts from US forces in Britain	30	42
Other receipts†	40	32
Sales of military equipment	670	834
Private expenditure by US forces in Britain	(80)	95
Total credits	820	1,023

SOURCE: *Statement on Defence Estimates, 1977*, Cmnd 6735; figure in brackets is an own estimate.
* Includes contributions to infrastructure projects, R & D levies, and contributions to international defence organizations.
† Includes such items as R & D levies.

This juxtaposition of credits and debits is to some extent misleading, since the item 'sales of military equipment' is not, strictly speaking, directly dependent on the scale of UK military expenditure. How would a reduction in UK military spending affect both the credit and debit sides? Certainly, under some of the options discussed in this study, the cost of stationing troops abroad would fall. (There would, of course, still be some balance of payments cost to their maintenance in this country.) The cost of purchases of military equipment would also be reduced. The effect that expenditure cuts might have on sales of military equipment would depend – among other things – on whether the recommendations about arms sales made elsewhere in this study were accepted. However, one of the contentions of this study is that, given time, the resources used at present in the production of arms for export could very well be transferred to the production of other engineering goods for export, and that the credits from this item could consequently be replaced.

Conclusion
It may be argued that the economic considerations which arise from a discussion of defence expenditure tend to overlook the general benefits inherent in such forms of expenditure. Such benefits would, it is suggested, relate to the need for domestic

security, global considerations of bargaining strength, protection of overseas commercial interests and so forth, as well as the need to maintain full employment when there is ideological resistance to non-military forms of public expenditure, and other matters relating to international obligations. These questions are considered in detail in the following chapters, but even at this stage the economic problems raised pose some fundamental questions about the extent to which the British economy, and those who create the wealth of our country, can and should be expected to bear the burden of excessive levels of defence expenditure.

Mary Kaldor sums up the nature of the inherent problems which have led to the situation in which the defence sector plays such a dominant role in the economy in these words:

'In some senses, the growth of defence spending can be seen as a symptom of the anarchy of our economic system. Partly because of the inherently subjective nature of strategic thinking and partly because of the unwillingness to admit the need for direct control over the economy, defence has come to be seen as a convenient instrument for economic policy-making – creating jobs, saving companies, and supporting the institutions of technology. At the same time, defence production has acquired a momentum of its own, exercising, in turn, an undue influence on military decision-making.'[21]

Such a momentum is built into the very structure of the decision-making system of the defence hierarchy, and has become so entrenched that any attempt to break away from this stultified manner of thinking will meet considerable resistance. Nevertheless, the fact is that the diversion of resources for the purposes of military production has proved inefficient in stimulating employment and exports, or generating new technology, and may even have helped to accelerate the process of industrial decline. It is also worth emphasizing that military expenditure is a particularly inefficient tool for demand management: because it is capital intensive, it has very little employment effect, and since the lead times for projects are so long, it cannot be used for stabilization policy. There is therefore an urgent need to reassess priorities and to see defence spending in its true context as a parasite on the economy as a whole.

If a true reassessment is to take place it must start with a genuine re-examination of future equipment requirements. It should also look towards an abandonment of the principle of independent viability, and hence of profit maximization for armament manufacture, to ensure that military requirements are not subordinated to the needs of the industry. The public ownership of the aerospace and shipbuilding industry is an important first step in this direction. Finally, there must be a fundamental restructuring throughout the defence industry, as any measures which would otherwise be attempted could only lead either to unemployment of workers and their equipment or to preserving the very structure which has proved so resistant to change in the past. The potential for the orderly conversion of the defence industries exists today. But the problem of industrial decline is of a structural nature, so the failure to take basic decisions about restructuring will surely lead to a situation in which there is even less room for manoeuvre.

Notes and References
 1. Second Report from the Expenditure Committee, Session 1974–5, 'The Defence Review Proposals', HC 259.
 2. Appendix IX: M. Kaldor, 'Defence Cuts and the Defence Industry'. The calculations are based on estimates made by the Stockholm International for Peace Research Institute (SIPRI) of the real resource cost in 1973 US dollars of individual aircraft. Warship costs are based on sources provided by the Annual Appropriation Accounts; *Janes Fighting Ships Annual*.
 3. Derek Wood, *Project Cancelled*, Macdonald's and Janes, London, 1975.
 4. J. R. Kurth, 'Why We Buy the Weapons We Do', *Foreign Policy*, No. 11, Summer 1973.
 5. Dr Michael Checinski, 'The Cost of Armament Production and the Profitability of Armament Export in Comecon Countries', The Hebrew University of Jerusalem, the Soviet and East-European Research Centre, Research Paper No. 10, Jerusalem, November 1974.
 6. Evidence of Vice-Admiral Clayton, Fifth Report from the Committee on Public Accounts, Session 1975–6, HCP 556.
 7. Appendix IX in the full report.
 8. Report of the Controller and Auditor-General, Appropriation Session 1975–6.
 9. See Appendix IX for a history of this project, which shows the high degree of similarity between the TSR-2 and the Tornado experience.
10. Arthur Reed, *Britain's Aircraft Industry, What Went Right? What Went Wrong?*, Dent, London, 1973, p. 114.
11. David Greenwood, 'Budgeting for Defence', *RUSI*, 1972, p. 7.
12. Appendix VIII: Ron Smith, 'The Resource Cost of Military Expenditure'.
13. Ministry of Defence, Written Answers, *Hansard*, 19 October 1976.
14. Appendix VIII. Smith describes the method used to produce the conclusion like this: 'This hypothesis was put into an operational form as a regression of the share of investment on the share of

military expenditure in GDP. Our theory would suggest that the slope coefficient should be −1. This was confirmed both by a time series regression for the UK, and a cross-section regression for 14 NATO countries. The results did not seem to be sensitive to the source of data, sample of countries within NATO, or the choice of time period. However, some qualifications had to be made with respect to exports in the immediate post-war period in the UK and with respect to intra-country regressions for some other NATO members. It also appeared that there were a number of areas which deserved further investigation.' A further discussion of this theory is to be found in R. P. Smith, 'Military Expenditure and Capitalism', *Cambridge Journal of Economics*, No. 1, 1977.

15. Based on a capital/output ratio of 3 (possibly a rather favourable figure for the UK).
16. This is the conclusion of the Shipbuilding Inquiry Committee 1956–66 Report ('The Geddes Report'), Cmnd 2937; see p. 129.
17. *Daily Telegraph*, 15 December 1976
18. Sources for totals: Military – Cmnd 6735; Agriculture – *Agriculture Research Council Report 1975–76*; Medical – *Labour Research*, May 1977.
19. *Input–Output Tables of the UK*, Department of Industry, 1975.
20. Kurt Rothschild, 'Military Expenditure, Exports and Growth', *Kyklos*, vol. XXVI, 1973.
21. M. Kaldor, 'Defence, Industrial Capacity and the Economy', paper submitted to the LP–NEC Defence Study Group.

4

THE STRATEGIC AND POLITICAL
IMPLICATIONS OF DEFENCE CUTS

The strategic and political implications of
defence cuts should not be seen in a purely national context. The
modern world is a dangerous place. The advanced industrial
countries devote increasing resources to the development and
manufacture of means of destruction; poor countries are buying
more conventional armaments; the risks of nuclear proliferation
are hideous; new technologies are spreading. How might British
defence cuts mitigate these dangers, and how could they contribute positively to international security? This is as important a
question as the negative one of how we can cut defence spending
without affecting national security.

Obviously the strategic and political implications of defence
cuts will depend on how they are carried out – the concrete
items affected and the co-ordination of defence and arms control
policies with those of other countries. The three main ways
considered here in which defence cuts might be carried out are
by no means mutually exclusive.

First, our allies might decide to take over or finance some of
our current military commitments. This would result in some
change in the balance of power within NATO.

Secondly, we might try to adopt more cost-effective methods of
carrying out current military functions. This could be possible
through less emphasis on sophisticated expensive weapon plat-
forms like Tornado and a more efficient use of new technologies.

51

Again, this would primarily affect relations with our allies and would depend on how they viewed such a change of tactics.

Thirdly, we might reduce real capabilities in the expectation that this would represent a significant contribution to détente and arms control.

Whatever the practical outcomes of these proposals, the strategic and political consequences of a £1,825 million cut in British military spending must be placed in the context of total military spending in the NATO countries with whom we share a common defence pact. In this perspective we find that a cut of £1,825 million would represent a gross reduction of less than 2 per cent in total spending.[1] So the strategic consequences of this action should not be overstated.

Before discussing ways and means by which defence cuts could be achieved 'painlessly', we need to examine critically the whole basis of prevalent strategic assumptions in the Ministry of Defence and elsewhere. It is not proposed to put forward an alternative strategic scenario, but rather to identify the problems inherent in current assumptions about the nature of the Soviet threat, and therefore to find a more rational basis for decision-making on military questions.

What is the Nature of the Soviet 'Threat'?

During a debate in the House of Commons on the 1977 Defence White Paper, Sir Ian Gilmour, the Conservative front bench spokesman on Defence, asked the Secretary of State whether there was really 'no evidence that the Soviets have aggressive intentions? If he really believes that', he continued, 'will he explain why the Russians are devoting all that effort to bring about that (military) explosion in their offensive capabilities?'[2] At a later stage in the debate, the Conservatives returned to the offensive in the shape of Mr Winston Churchill, who told the House that 'the only valid yardstick' by which to measure the necessary level of defence expenditure was an estimation of 'the perceived level of threat . . . Despite the ritual howls for uni-lateral defence cuts,' continued Mr Churchill, '. . . it is signi-ficant that no Hon. Member, even from the left wing of their party, is suggesting that the Soviet threat has diminished.'[3] The comment in the White Paper which seems to have excited Conservative fears appears to be: 'There is no evidence to suggest that NATO's policy of deterrence is failing and that the Warsaw Pact is contemplating aggression against NATO.'[4] It is our view

52

that this is a perfectly reasonable assessment and that there is plenty of evidence to support it.

In analysing the nature of the strategic problems facing this country, we start from the assumption that if there were a genuine possibility of foreign invasion it would be necessary to devote the greater part of our resources to repelling such an attack. In the current situation, however, we are constantly being told that the source of potential aggression is the USSR. If this is so, then it is necessary to consider the problem in terms of:

(a) Soviet intentions;
(b) Soviet interests; and
(c) Soviet abilities.

(a) *Soviet Intentions*

It is a common military aphorism that one should look only at capabilities and not at intentions, since capabilities can be observed and intentions cannot. Unfortunately, this is not a logical suggestion. If we simply considered capabilities, we might as well prepare ourselves for attack from the USA or from the USA and USSR in combination, or from France and the Federal Republic of Germany in combination. We do not do this because, although the USA has the capability, we do not believe it has the intention.

The first point to make about Soviet intentions is that decision-makers in the USSR no more form a monolithic bloc with a single set of intentions than do decision-makers in Britain or the USA. There are very real and well-documented divisions within the bureaucracies of the Soviet and Warsaw Pact countries, and their attitudes tend to follow a fairly predictable pattern. Put broadly, the most influential groupings would appear to be the Party hierarchy (probably rather more 'dove-like' than 'hawkish'), the military and heavy industry (tending towards 'hawkishness'), the state bureaucracy, light industry and agriculturalists (tending towards 'dovishness'), and the internal security apparatus whose tendencies in this respect are hard to define.[5] Within these groupings there are further sub-divisions and divergences, and shifts in the internal balance of power often cannot be explained except by reference to these smaller sub-groups. Furthermore, Soviet decision-makers are very much influenced by Western actions. Therefore if the West were seen to be reducing its military strength, the 'dovish' factions would be strengthened, and *vice versa* if Western military activity was increasing.

Despite the complexity of the question, a general pattern of indications of Soviet intentions can be identified. The recent Helsinki Conference on Security and Cooperation in Europe is a good starting point to examine this question. The Soviet objective at Helsinki, one which Moscow has long sought to achieve, was to obtain international recognition of the *status quo* in Eastern Europe, an area which marks the confines of Soviet territorial ambitions. In return, they have had to offer very limited concessions on the question of human rights, a gesture which was aimed at the West, as well as recognizing the growing tensions in the over-extended 'empire' of Eastern Europe.

Helsinki demonstrates the depth of Soviet concern to stabilize the situation in the territories already under Soviet hegemony. It reflects their intention to consolidate their existing sphere of dominance rather than any drive to create fresh problems by extending territory. Russian expansion is more concerned with the creation of a limited land-based 'cordon sanitaire' on her Western front than with territorial adventures further afield.

We should not, however, underestimate the deeply felt desire of the USSR to achieve parity with the United States in all fields, and particularly in arms. 'Despite years of Herculean effort and indisputable Soviet success in many fields of strategic development,' writes Robert Kaiser, 'the new American President still claims "superiority". It is not difficult to imagine how the Pentagon would react if it had presided over a similar history.'[6] The struggle for parity has been a central characteristic of the world military situation. The general pattern has been for the USSR to follow US technological developments with a varying time-lag. Writing in the US *Foreign Affairs* journal, Alexander R. Vershbow comments: 'The US has too often been the leader (or culprit) in the introduction of new, more deadly technologies.'[7]

The USSR trailed in the development of atomic weapons; in the 1960s it lagged in building up the number of inter-continental missiles (despite the famous, and mythical, 'missile gap' of the late 1950s); it was several years behind in the development of MIRV (multiple independently targeted re-entry vehicles). And now the United States threatens to bound ahead again with the long-range cruise missile, with its sophisticated computer guidance and 'incredibly high degree of accuracy'.[8] The occasions in the post-war period when Soviet troops have actually taken military action outside their borders were when they thought that their hold on their Eastern European colonial empire was threatened.

54

In world-wide interventions they have been far more cautious than the Americans. There were no Soviet troops in Korea; none in Vietnam; there is no Soviet analogue to the landing of American marines in Lebanon. They even came late to the supply of arms as a technique of trying to win the allegiance of Third World countries – the first supply of arms outside the Soviet bloc was not until 1955.

There are compelling reasons for regarding the USSR as basically a *status quo* power in Europe. Its pressure has always been for the legitimization of the frontiers existing at the end of the Second World War, and for the acceptance of the dividing-line across Germany. It must be remembered that, during the long abortive negotiations over a peace treaty, it was the Western powers who refused to accept the division of Germany, and in Soviet eyes the rearmament of West Germany could well have looked like the prelude to an armed Western intervention to reunite Germany, an alarming prospect given the devastation suffered by the USSR during the Second World War. Indeed, the European policies of the Soviet Union since 1945 contrast heavily with the policies of Germany up to 1939 (which are often cited as an ominous parallel); Soviet pressure, culminating in the campaign leading up to the Helsinki Conference, has been for acceptance of the way things are, whereas it was clear, from the Ruhr occupation on, that the objectives of Nazi Germany were of a different order entirely.

In many parts of the world outside Europe the USSR, like other Great Powers, has given political, material and military support to various organizations and countries but always in pursuit of her own national interest.

Those who are committed to the assumption that the USSR is an enormous threat are forced to view this passivity and this defence of the *status quo* as an enormous trick. Western Europe will be lulled into complacency and, like a thunderbolt from the clear blue sky, the Eastern hordes will swoop across north Germany. This scenario contains severe military problems: even if the USSR had a standing-start attack capability it is most doubtful whether she would wish, or have the capability, to sustain an attack into hostile territory.

Those who argue that Soviet policy is one big trick often assume that Moscow's 'ideological struggle' contradicts and exposes its détente policy. A more dispassionate approach suggests that the Soviet leaders fear – probably rightly – that easing international tension will increase pressure to relax domestic

55

controls; thus, precisely because they cannot utterly control the population, they are determined to prevent the penetration of foreign ideas and influence into Soviet society. In short, the intensification of the ideological campaign is 'related exclusively to internal needs and situations and has exceedingly little to do with Soviet international behaviour'.[9] It is no evidence of aggressive intentions abroad, and in no way supports the 'con-trick' theory of Soviet policy.

(b) *Soviet Interests*
Indications of Soviet intentions become more readily understood once the question, 'What does the USSR stand to gain by invading Western Europe?' has been answered. The reply does not demand an analysis of Soviet benevolence, but rather a practical consideration of whether such an action could produce beneficial results.

As we have noted, the USSR's main present concern is the preservation of her hegemony over the Eastern European Warsaw Pact states – recent events in Poland and Czechoslovakia serve to emphasize the costs and difficulties of Soviet control, as well as the vast problems inherent in deploying thousands of garrison troops outside her own borders. It seems unrealistic to assume that the USSR would wish to compound these problems by taking on the additional problems of a conquest of Western Europe.

There is also a school of thought which accepts that the USSR does not intend to attack us, but argues that it will tend to use its superior military strength to 'lean on' Western Europe in other ways. It is very difficult to discover what ways this school has in mind. First of all, the simple possession of greater military strength is not much help unless one is prepared to incur the odium of a clear and definite threat to use it. And if the USSR is prepared to use its superior military strength to lean on European countries, why has it not done so in areas where that superior strength is obvious? Why has it not used it in negotiations with Sweden, for example? Why has it not used it with Yugoslavia? Indeed, why does it not lean on Britain in the matter of extending fishing limits to two hundred miles, from which it stands to lose considerably?

The reason is that military power does not provide unqualified and simple advantages to any state, and that it is in Soviet interests to pursue a policy of détente rather than of aggression.

The USSR's primary objectives in the European arena, which

underlie its advocacy of détente, hinge on the maintenance of the *status quo*, not its disturbance.[10] It has long sought Western recognition of the inviolability of existing frontiers and non-recourse to force; acceptance of the division of Germany; and expanded economic cooperation between East and West. It is relying heavily on the importation of advanced Western technology and the impact of foreign trade to stimulate a growth-rate which has been declining since the early 1960s. The Soviet leadership is heavily committed to economic growth and steadily rising living standards.

Until recently, the USSR has relied heavily on quantitative sources of growth – the deployment of increasing quantities of the basic factors of production. However, since resources are not available to power quantitative economic growth at the necessary rate, future increases in Soviet growth rate will depend upon a more efficient integration of basic factors of production – upon qualitative growth. The over-centralized Soviet economic system, dominated by bureaucracies which make no adequate response to consumer demand, acts as a drag upon productivity, and rather than contemplate a radical overhaul of the system, the Soviet leadership seems to prefer increasing imports of sophisticated Western technology to foster qualitative growth.[11] Dependence upon Western technology – as the Soviet leaders, no doubt reluctantly, accept – draws the Soviet economy into the capitalist-dominated world economic system. Above all – and this may well be a point in its favour for many Soviet policy-makers – it means that the country's economic interests are best served by, and are indeed becoming reliant upon, improved political relations with the West.

The hallmark of the Soviet leadership, and the main cause of its neurotic reaction to any sign of internal dissent, are caution and conservatism. Both within and without the borders of the USSR, there is a clear *status quo* that the Soviet leaders wish to preserve. Many of the apparent ambiguities in their détente policy stem from occasional contradictions between the demands of their internal and external policies.

Détente, in other words, symbolizes the growing interdependence between East and West. Ironically, it is also the very existence of outward hostility between the two super-powers which holds together their respective spheres of influence. Victory or defeat, total destruction or total reconciliation, would destroy their domination and hegemony.

(c) *Soviet Abilities*

The USSR possesses massive and well-equipped armed forces. The fact that the country devotes about 12 per cent of the Gross National Product[12] to defence, and that she is developing sophisticated weapons delivery systems like the Backfire and the Foxbat, are the main reasons why there is concern about Soviet military intentions. The military balance is discussed in more detail below, but it will be useful here to indicate certain influential factors which could affect our perception of the balance.

First, it should be emphasized that whereas the West identifies its sole potential aggressor as the Warsaw Pact countries, the USSR sees itself as facing two threats: from China as well as the West. The USSR is consequently obliged to divide its deployment of military resources accordingly. The Chinese, with a population of 850 million and a military force of some 3·5 million incorporating a nuclear capability, are seen as a serious opponent. Military planners in Moscow are constantly exercised by the fear of a two-front war. As a respected American author on Soviet diplomatic history has written: 'The rapid buildup of the Soviet stockpile and delivery system in the 1960s must be understood as reflecting the need not only to reduce America's superiority but to establish a crushing Soviet superiority over China's budding nuclear power.'[13] Similarly, a Rand Corporation expert on Soviet military policy has stated that it is 'a real question whether the Soviet leadership still feels that the primary military threat to Soviet interests is posed by [the West] or . . . [by] Communist China'.[14]

Apart from the Chinese dimension, there is also the lesser factor of the deployment of Soviet forces in Eastern Europe. The fact that Soviet troops are virtually, if not actually, garrison troops, means that they cannot readily be moved to another front. Indeed, any movement of troops could have severe internal repercussions. There is also some debate on the degree of homogeneity within the Warsaw Pact. While the NATO countries could almost certainly be expected to act in concert, several observers (notably the CIA in the 1960s) have questioned the extent to which the troops of some Eastern European countries could be relied upon to fight outside their own borders. As the former US Defence Secretary, Robert McNamara, remarked: '. . . we are no longer convinced that the East European forces, which constitute more than half of the Warsaw Pact's combat ready strength in Central Europe, would be fully effective in an unprovoked attack on NATO.'[15]

The Military Balance

The military balance is open to a great variety of interpretations; consequently, perceptions of this balance are highly subjective. Official sources (concerned to raise defence budgets) tend to emphasize Warsaw Pact strength. Other sources (including those in semi-official circles) present a different picture. It does not take great imagination to suppose that the Soviet Ministry of Defence's presentation of the military balance is different again. The picture can change according to the way in which the geographical area is defined, or qualitative factors are taken into account, and so on.

But a more important reason for not giving undue weight to detailed presentations of the military balance is the fact that they too often imply that security is a technical matter (and, indeed, a matter of how well you can do your sums). Yet this is fallacious, for security is created by economic strength and political will as well as military power. The balance can be conceived of as relatively stable, and impervious to minor shifts in one direction or another, since it is impossible to calculate it in any but the crudest terms. While it may be true that détente rests on a military balance which precludes the use of force in East–West relations, it is wrong to see the military relationship as the only (or even the dominant) one.

Methods of assessing the military balance are themselves a matter of concern. On both sides, hawks and doves are involved in the process of assessing and drawing conclusions from the state of the military balance; the data themselves thus become matter for political dispute.

It is relatively easy for a hawk to justify the case for an unlimited arms race. All that is necessary is to argue that the nation should be ready for the 'worst case'. With two sides doing a 'worst-case' analysis, there is, of course, no limit to an arms race. The position of the doves on either side is weaker. They can point to the insanity of the process, an argument which never sounds as powerful as it should, and to the waste of valuable resources. But the momentum behind military policies on both sides is formidable.

It is therefore unfortunate that most sources of information are in the hands of the hawks. The people who advise the civil power on the size of the military threat are the military themselves; this inevitably leads to bias, since the military, like all other bureaucracies, are obviously looking for justifications to increase their resources. There is nothing particularly malign about the tend-

59

ency of the military to select the facts which fit their cause. All such groups tend to do this. In most cases, however, there are good sources of counter-information. But in this case – the assessment of the threat from the potential enemy – reliable independent sources of information are almost non-existent.

It is nevertheless essential to try to gain a more objective perspective of the balance of military power. Such an attempt necessarily involves a consideration of the rather repetitive numbers game, and even though this is an unsatisfactory way of calculating the comparative effectiveness of opposing military forces, it is on numbers that much of the public justification for defence policy depends. In the sections which follow we look at the arguments as they relate to each branch of the armed forces.

(a) *Naval forces*

The main concern of those who talk about Soviet naval expansion is not its absolute size. The numbers of ships have not actually changed in recent years, but rather has the Soviet navy changed from being a coastal defence force to an ocean-going fleet. It is suggested that the USSR is aiming for an offensive capability to enable it to intervene and interdict Western shipping. Yet the evidence for this viewpoint is scant. The Soviet naval infantry is extremely small, numbering 14,500, and has been declining. The USSR has no sea-based air power to give cover for intervention. The new VTOL aircraft carriers are of little use in any role but anti-submarine warfare. Finally, the USSR has a very limited sea-based support system, and her overseas naval facilities, particularly following political shifts in Egypt and Somalia, are quite inadequate. Some authorities have explained the changed deployment of the Soviet fleet as a response to the US nuclear attack carriers which appeared in the mid 1950s and Polaris submarines which appeared in the early 1960s.[16] Moreover, the Soviet press emphasizes the way in which naval 'visibility' provides a political underpinning to détente.

It is this last factor which is probably the primary cause of concern over the Soviet Navy for NATO's leaders. According to Michael Klare:

By gaining 'new visibility in areas of the world which have traditionally been within the Western sphere of influence' (to use Admiral Rectanus' words), Moscow has called into question the invulnerability of Western fleets there and thus their utility as instruments of coercion and influence. Thus, it is not Western *shipping* that is threatened by Soviet naval deployments, but Washington's strategy for continued Western hegemony in remote Third World areas.[17] (Italics in original.)

(b) *Ground forces*

The 1976 Defence White Paper states categorically that 'in conventional ground and air forces, the imbalance in Central Europe has moved further in the Warsaw Pact's favour'.[18] It is significant that this kind of grandiose claim is not repeated in the White Paper for 1977.

Above all else, the problem troubling Ministry of Defence strategists seems to be the sheer size of the 1·8 million-strong Soviet army. Yet the total army strength of European NATO nations, together with US troops stationed in Europe, is about 2 million, and the USSR must also be uncomfortably aware that the Chinese army numbers some 3 million. Thus the size of the Soviet army does not seem over-large given the size of its potential adversaries. Much has been made of Warsaw Pact numerical superiority in the European theatre; the presentation has often been misleading, occasionally descending to the level of counting up divisions without mentioning that the average NATO division strength in the theatre is considerably greater than the Warsaw Pact average strength.

The International Institute for Strategic Studies has estimated that NATO has 635,000 combat and direct support troops available in Northern and Central Europe, while the Warsaw Pact has an estimated 910,000. A recently published survey of forces shows a different picture, estimating effective NATO strength at 725,000 and Warsaw Pact strength at 780,000.[19] This disparity is probably accounted for by the fact that the Warsaw Pact uses military people to perform functions which are carried out in NATO by civilians. The IISS figures do not reflect this position (although they do qualify their figures in the accompanying text). However, this superiority is not of itself of a magnitude likely to be essential for a conquest of Western Europe; the NATO figure excludes all French forces, and also US 'dual-based' brigades which could be flown in relatively quickly. In Southern Europe, the numerical advantage is NATO's, by 540,000 to 395,000.[20] The Warsaw Pact does, however, have an advantage in terms of reinforcement, as a land link between its forces ensures a more speedy availability of heavy equipment. Nevertheless, the picture is by no means as alarming as the more extreme 'worst-case' analysts would have us believe, and limited reductions or increases on either side would affect the analysis only minimally, if at all.

Besides the concern about manpower, there is alarm over Soviet tank superiority. The factual basis of this assertion is undeniable. However, a purely numerical comparison is misleading. The former US Assistant Secretary of Defence, Alan C. Enthoven, shows why this is so:

> It is not clear that this numerical superity in Pact tanks is a decisive advantage. It reflects Soviet tradition, which stresses tanks heavily. NATO armies have deliberately chosen to place less emphasis on tanks than do the Soviets. We could increase the emphasis on tanks if we thought the total effectiveness of our forces would be increased thereby . . . Studies show that the NATO tanks and anti-tank weapons have a high kill potential against the Pact tank force . . . In addition, one must consider the additional large tanks kill potential of our tactical aircraft.[21]

The decreased emphasis on tanks by NATO is, in our opinion, a proper decision; and it does make the concern about inferiority in tank numbers seem a little misdirected. If NATO's anti-tank weapons are effective, then the tank balance matters less, quantitatively or qualitatively. Finally, it should be emphasized that NATO sees itself as having different strategic objectives from the Warsaw Pact; its forces should not therefore be a copy of Warsaw Pact forces. A military force should be structured according to its own objectives, not according to some other force's assumed objectives.[22]

(c) *Air force*
There is little conclusive evidence to reveal the true balance between the rival air forces. Although the Warsaw Pact appears to have maintained a consistent numerical superiority in tactical aircraft, much of this is accounted for by its far greater numbers of interceptor aircraft for air defence. In 1973, the Pentagon estimated that, in an actual European battle, given likely reinforcement, the tactical air forces of each side would be 'about even at 5,000 to 6,000 each'.[23]

(d) *The military budget*
There is an increasing tendency for military planners to cite disparities in the military budget as a means of comparing

military strength. Such comparisons have a poor track record for accuracy, particularly with regard to Soviet figures from Western sources (and no doubt *vice versa*, if we had access to this information). The point is, however, that the level of spending tells us very little about what is being purchased. The whole process of making budget comparisons is obscure at every level, and is so contentious that firm conclusions are difficult to reach. The sources of information range from the CIA data included in the *Military Balance* to alternative figures from the Stockholm International Peace Research Institute (SIPRI). The problem is illustrated by a comparison of Soviet military expenditure between 1970–75, the CIA estimating that it has *increased* by 4 to 5 per cent, and another American source estimating a *9 per cent increase*. SIPRI, on the other hand, estimates a *fall* of 3 per cent.[24]

The differences between these various estimates can be explained by different methods of calculation. The CIA estimate is an attempt to calculate how much it would cost the US government to 'buy' the Soviet military establishment, in dollars, at American prices. The calculation immediately falls into awesome methodological problems, since conscription makes Soviet military manpower much cheaper than American manpower, whereas general technology is cheaper to the USA than to the USSR. If the calculation is reversed and the rouble cost to the Soviet government of 'buying' the American military establishment is estimated, the US appears the bigger spender. As a US congressman, Les Aspin, points out, since the American arms inventory includes items much more sophisticated than the Soviets have (in the field of computers and advanced electronics), a calculation such as this is bound to *underestimate* the cost to the USSR of 'replicating the physical dimensions and operational capabilities' of the US military. As he rightly concludes, 'the answer to the question, "who is spending more on defence?" depends on the price system used.'[25] The SIPRI figures are based on the official Soviet budget, taking account of hidden costs included in the Soviet science budget and of the difficulties of choosing an appropriate exchange rate.

Yet another method, used by the American source quoted above, would include an unaccounted-for residual in the output of the machine-building and metal-working industries.

(e) *The Nuclear Balance*
The USA is estimated to have approximately 8,530 strategic nuclear warheads, the USSR approximately 3,250.[26] Various

63

other measures of the balance qualify this appearance of an American lead. For example, in megatonnage the USSR is believed to have a considerable lead, though this is partly offset by the greater average accuracy of the US arsenal. It is extremely difficult to arrive at an adequate assessment of the relative capabilities of the two forces, and this is in any case really a rather pointless exercise. As Henry Kissinger once asked, 'What in the name of God is strategic superiority? What do you do with it?'[27] The only kind of strategic superiority which would have meaning is if one side were to develop a first-strike capability – the ability to destroy all or most of the other side's strategic nuclear weapons. Neither side possesses this ability; nor is it likely to for some time, if ever; nor is it in any way desirable for either to seek to attain it. Short of that, the staggering degree of overkill in each side's nuclear arsenal makes talk of strategic superiority meaningless.

Britain possesses 192 strategic nuclear warheads on Polaris missiles, a trivial figure in comparison to the super-powers' arsenals and evidence enough that the British contribution to the strategic nuclear balance is irrelevant.

Although the figures are not known with any precision, it is generally estimated that NATO's European theatre nuclear forces consist of about 7,000 tactical nuclear weapons for delivery by aircraft, missile and artillery, or in the form of atomic demolition munitions. The Warsaw Pact is believed to have about 3,500 tactical nuclear weapons.[28] Recently both sides have strengthened their theatre nuclear forces: NATO through the increased numbers of American F-111 bombers based in Britain, and the Warsaw Pact through the development of the SS-X-20 medium-range missile.

The study group views this build-up with alarm. There is already a considerable degree of overkill in each side's forces: it seems impossible that NATO could have 7,000 potential targets, or anywhere near that number, for its theatre nuclear forces; and while the Warsaw Pact has fewer weapons in this category, they are believed to be more powerful though considerably less accurate. Any war involving the use of large numbers of these tactical weapons would have, so far as Europe is concerned, strategic effects killing millions of people and rendering vast areas uninhabitable. At the Mutual Force Reduction talks in Vienna, NATO proposed withdrawing a large number of tactical nuclear weapons in exchange for the Warsaw Pact withdrawing a number of tanks. This would seem to be a recognition that NATO has tactical nuclear superiority (for what it is worth), and that it has more tactical nuclear weapons than it can possibly need.

The nuclear arms race presents an incredible risk of warfare in the modern age. To gain some impression of the size of the problem, we should remember that the atomic bomb dropped on Hiroshima unleashed an equivalent of between 13,000 and 20,000 tons of TNT. It has been estimated that the USA has warheads aimed at the USSR with an equivalent TNT explosive power of some 4,200,000,000 tons, and that the Soviet arsenal is even larger.[29]

After examining the problem of making comparisons about the military balance, Dan Smith comments:

Most of the conventional comparisons of military force between NATO and the Warsaw Pact are very dubious, serving to confuse rather than clarify. No clear picture can be provided and firmly held. So much depends upon estimation and interpretation of disputed data, that only the most limited conclusions are really possible.[30]

We have considered some of the problems of examining the military balance. We do not conclude that the NATO countries are militarily either stronger or weaker than those of the Warsaw Pact. Any reconsideration of expenditure priorities must incorporate a reconsideration of both the purpose of our military expenditure and the strategic context. If calculations of essential expenditure are to be based on the magnitude of the Soviet threat, a rather more objective method of making a true assessment is needed. There seems to be nothing in this area to dissuade the Labour Party from its policy of reducing military expenditure.

The Arms Race, Détente and Arms Control
This study's proposals for reducing defence expenditure are put forward during a period of intensive international reassessments of political and strategic questions. The contradictory pressures of an escalating arms race, as against a growing awareness of the need for arms control, are tempered by the emerging political environment in a period of East–West détente. While it is possible to identify some areas of achievement on human rights and trade matters in East–West relations, it is not possible to point to any significant success in the field of military détente.

Seen in global terms, it is clear that not even a reduction in

British military expenditure of around £1,800 million would radically alter the overall picture, though such a move should be viewed in the context of these developments.

Détente between East and West is a far more complex and ambiguous relationship than that which prevailed during the Cold War. The argument advanced by each side that a balance of military power provides the basis for détente presupposes, in the West, that the USSR is fundamentally aggressive; and in the USSR that the West is fundamentally aggressive. At the same time, each side accepts that common interests exist in avoiding confrontation and extending economic relations. These ambiguities are deeply rooted, not only in international relations but also in domestic institutions. Disturbing though they are, they are preferable to the certainties of the Cold War. Moreover, there are powerful reasons why the two super-powers should wish to maintain this ambiguous relationship, and in this their interests are, to a considerable extent, complementary.

The arms race is not merely continuing; it is becoming both more extensive and more intensive. Three worrying features may be discerned. First, since 1973 there have been substantial real increases in military spending in both NATO and Warsaw Pact countries, in particular in the USA, France, Britain, the two Germanies, Poland and the USSR. Secondly, there has been a proliferation of military technologies of all kinds. The trade in conventional major weapons with the Third World has increased nearly five-fold over the past ten years. Six countries have now exploded nuclear devices, while a seventh, Israel, is widely believed to possess untested nuclear weapons. Since 1965, the number of countries capable of producing nuclear weapons at short notice has increased from six to twenty-two.[31] Thirdly, there have been major technological changes in non-nuclear weapons. The development of precision-guided munitions has received much attention, but while their defensive potential has been lauded, their development could provoke the development of new 'area suppression' weapons, such as napalm, binary gas weapons and environmental modification weapons. One more hopeful sign in this respect is the new ENMOD treaty on the control of hostile uses of environmental modification techniques, which represents a limited but necessary first step towards reducing the dangers of environmental warfare.

Against this background, talks proceed in Vienna about mutual balanced force reductions, the super-powers discuss strategic arms limitation (SALT) and the nuclear powers engage in attempts to prevent nuclear proliferation. Tangentially, the reduction of military tension was on the agenda of the Helsinki Security and Cooperation Conference, and is on that of the follow-up Belgrade Review. The striking fact which emerges from all these high-level deliberations is the lack of progress towards a reduction of military forces; nor, with the possible exception of the SALT talks, is any real progress likely. This suggests that while international negotiations may provide the *forum* in which arms control agreements are reached, they will not be the *agency* for achieving effective arms limitation, because they do not tackle the domestic sources of the problem. Defence cuts, by weakening domestic pressures, can make a major contribution to arms control. As we have said, East–West relations are complex and ambiguous, but it is most unlikely that even swingeing defence cuts would make these relations unstable. But defence cuts might well contribute to a policy of emphasizing the cooperative rather than the hostile elements in the relationship.

British unilateral action will not in itself (obviously) alter dramatically the course of arms control talks. It will, however, be a contribution to something more productive than long-drawn-out international gatherings, and it is an opportunity for Britain to play a role in bringing about a less tense international climate.

Options for Reducing Defence Expenditure

As we have demonstrated, there are, at the very least, wide areas of contention in prevalent strategic thinking. Questioning some of the deeply held assumptions of military planners shows that, if there are to be reductions in military spending, there is more room for manoeuvre than might be expected. We now look at the strategic and political implications of the various options for cuts suggested in Chapter 3. Once again, the options discussed are not prescriptive. There is an infinite variety of combinations of cuts that could be made, and what is involved here is an illustrative exercise, assessing the nature and consequences of the kind of changes which a significant reshaping of our military effort would require.[32]

In Chapter 2, we showed how a remodelling of the armed forces might include a mixture of the following alternatives:

1. Phasing out Polaris.
2. Paying off *Ark Royal, Hermes, Fearless* and *Intrepid,* can-

celling the second and third ASW Cruisers and Sea Harrier, running down patrol submarine activity and 'stretching' building programmes for fleet submarines, destroyers and frigates.
3. Reducing BAOR to about 30,000 men, with appropriate equipment reductions and a proportional cut in home forces to reflect a reduced requirement for rotating units to and from BAOR.
4. Cancelling both versions of the multi-role combat aircraft, Tornado, with reductions in tankers and air transport, and increased expenditure on Harrier and Jaguar.

These options would have to be considered together with proportionate reductions in support programmes and the withdrawal of all ground forces stationed outside Europe.

1. *Polaris*
The option discussed is a progressive phasing-out of all provision for the Polaris force.

As we have seen, the contribution of Polaris to the strategic nuclear balance is trivial; there is, in fact, some doubt, from the Pentagon at least,[33] about the role of Polaris in NATO's strategic forces. The political arguments in favour of keeping Polaris have generally been more comprehensible than the military ones, though they owe much to lingering delusions of grandeur. Some have argued that there are dangers in abandoning Polaris and leaving France the sole strategic European nuclear power. Others suggest that retaining Polaris ensures the (already certain) commitment of the USA to NATO. If this latter argument implies that Britain scrapping Polaris would result in the USA leaving NATO, then it is absurd; and if it does not imply that, it is hard to see what it does mean.

There is no overwhelming financial advantage in phasing out Polaris, and our options therefore do not rule out maintaining the fleet for the rest of its natural 'life' (ten to thirteen years).[34] However, retaining Polaris must not be allowed in any way to undermine the clear commitment of the Labour Party and Government against developing a further generation of strategic nuclear weapons. In any case, the replacement of Polaris would impose a very severe burden of expenditure.

The study group has found, however, no compelling arguments against abandoning Polaris, and the opportunity might be taken to use the scrapping of Polaris to stimulate wider and faster moves towards arms reductions and disarmament. The attempt might fail, but if Polaris is to be abandoned because of the need to reduce military spending, and if there are no *adverse* consequences, then the attempt should be made to wring all possible advantage from the decision.[35]

2. *Naval General Purpose Forces*

Britain's navy, large by comparison with the navies of our European allies, is structured around big ships with deep-water, long-cruise ability. It provides 70 per cent of NATO's East Atlantic forces. The effect of the reductions proposed here would be to transform the structure of the Royal Navy. This would continue to fulfil its main roles, but without large surface ships, such as the new anti-submarine warfare (ASW) cruisers, and would abandon some roles, such as amphibious warfare, upon which less emphasis is already being placed.

There is a general consensus that the main naval threat to NATO in the areas in which the Royal Navy operates comes from the Soviet submarine forces, though there is also some concern about Soviet surface ships. However, it is not at all clear that the best way to counter this threat is the current strategy of using ASW task forces based around ASW cruisers. Not only are larger ships larger and more inviting targets, but their expense limits the total number of them available. A navy based on smaller ships would seem to offer an equally effective and cheaper way of carrying out the main tasks for which, if these proposals were adopted, the Royal Navy would be exclusively structured. Although the navy would lack both sea-borne aviation and amphibious warfare ability, its range of operations for the missions which should receive priority would not be changed.

3. *European Theatre Ground Forces*

The reduction of BAOR from 55,000 to 30,000 men is a major cut, but looks less significant in the overall context of NATO European ground forces. As a percentage of combat and direct support troops, it corresponds to a cut of 3·9 per cent in North and Central Europe, a 2·1 per cent cut in the whole of Europe, and a 3·4 per cent cut in the area covered by the Mutual Force Reduction talks. If French ground forces were also counted, the percentages would be lower. Directly proportionate equipment reductions might mean, for example, reducing the BAOR tank force from 650 to 350, corresponding to reductions of 4·3, 2·7 and 4·7 per cent in NATO tank forces in the same regions, again excluding French forces.[37]

If such reductions were undertaken, their effect on BAOR's combat strength might be lessened through further reorganization.[38] They could also profitably be accompanied by tactical alterations designed to take advantage of the new types of anti-tank guided weapons (ATGW) which seem likely to reduce the tactical advantages of tanks. The accuracy of ATGW, combined with modern sensor devices, could, it has been argued, provide an individual company with 'a greater anti-tank potential than a whole mechanized battalion before 1970'.[39] While it must be recognized that the effectiveness of ATGW is a subject for debate, it may be that their deployment, and appropriate tactical changes, would make possible a reduction of manpower without loss of defensive effectiveness. BAOR would then be a relatively small force, capable of strong mobile defence and based on small units which possessed the advantages of relative speed of movement and ease of concealment.[40]

Such changes in BAOR would, of course, have political repercussions (see below). Many will also argue that it would lower the nuclear threshold – hence, that in a conflict, nuclear weapons would have to be used earlier. This objection is based on the assumption that a limited war in Europe is possible. Yet this assumption seems questionable so long as tactical nuclear weapons are deployed widely in Europe. Those who are concerned about the nuclear threshold should focus on the size of the nuclear arsenal rather than on the consequences of marginal changes in conventional forces.

Finally, no discussion of British ground forces can ignore their major active role – that in Northern Ireland. It has not been within the study group's terms of reference to discuss this issue in any detail. Nevertheless it is clear that if the Northern Ireland role is to continue, there should be adequate provision for air transport so that, should a reduced BAOR be drawn on for some contingency in Northern Ireland, then the speedy return of troops to Germany remains practicable. On the other hand, reductions in this programme could go hand in hand with a major reassessment of the utilization of troops in Northern Ireland.

4. *Air Force General Purpose Forces*
The central feature of this option is the cancellation of the multi-role combat aircraft Tornado. The proposed reduction in air transport creates some difficulties, as air transport has already been reduced. Decisions about it should be made in the light of

the transport requirements of ground forces and the possibilities of commandeering civil aircraft.

Cancelling Tornado would effectively remove from the RAF one of its most important missions: long-range bombing. Missions which involve deep penetration of enemy air space have been made more difficult by the development of precision-guided surface-to-air missiles (SAMs), though terrain-following radar does make low-flying missions more feasible. Electronic counter-measures can also reduce the effectiveness of SAM, but it can be restored by the use of electronic counter-counter-measures. It may be argued that the expensive deep-penetration mission – whether to strike at airfields, troop concentrations, installations or cities – should not be a priority for a country like Britain which needs to cut back its military spending.

Also lost would be the Tornado air defence variant, which, together with SAM, is intended to provide air defence for the United Kingdom. The proposal in the event of Tornado cancellation would be to use Phantom as an air defence interceptor throughout the 1980s, with improvements to their Sparrow air-to-air missiles.

The consequent air force would be one whose priority missions would be battlefield interdiction and the attainment, so far as possible, of local air superiority over the battlefield. For the first of these the RAF has two fine aircraft, the Harrier and the Jaguar; the latter is also capable of tactical reconnaissance and air combat. Expenditure upon either or both could be increased if thought necessary. Limiting the RAF's roles in this way might in the future eliminate the need for multi-role aircraft, which are not only extremely expensive, but in general tend to perform less well than aircraft designed for specific tasks.[41] It may become possible to concentrate upon cheaper and more specialized aircraft.[42]

5. *Additional Cuts*
Reductions in support programmes would not involve political or military consequences apart from those already discussed. Reducing or removing overseas bases would have political consequences, but it is not clear what positive role these bases have. During the 1974 Cyprus crisis, British troops stationed on the island were confined to barracks. It is hard to see the point of stationing troops where they cannot be used.

Burden-sharing
A possible way of reducing British defence expenditure would

71

be to share the defence burden. The principles of collective burden-sharing are well established; they are the same principles which underlie progressive taxation. The *proportion* of resources devoted to a common purpose should be greater for the rich than for the poor. This principle is, of course, fully accepted, not only by the Labour Party but also by the Conservative Party in its approach to the taxation of incomes. The only question at issue is the degree of progressivenesss.

The same basic principles should apply in burden-sharing between countries which are devoting resources to a common purpose. Income per head in the United Kingdom is, at estimated purchasing-power parities, now some 25 per cent below income per head in Western Germany and France.[43] The gap is widening, and there is every indication that it will continue to widen. It widened further in 1976, when national output (at constant prices) is estimated to have risen 5 per cent in Germany, 4·5 per cent in France, but only 1 per cent in the United Kingdom. It is virtually certain that it will widen further in 1977, when national output is forecast to rise 5 per cent in Germany, 4 per cent in France and 1·5 per cent in the United Kingdom. Thus, year by year, it becomes more and more difficult for Britain to devote the same proportion of its resources as France and Germany for collective defence purposes, let alone a larger share. It is clearly time that we admitted to being a relatively poor country and had our share of the collective burden consequently adjusted. This argument is simple and straightforward, and it is a big argument. It is a manifest absurdity that, when we are so much poorer than France or Germany, we should be devoting a larger proportion of our resources than they are to military expenditure.[44]

Why then has the United Kingdom been so weak in putting forward in NATO this essentially open-and-shut case? There are a number of reasons. First, politicians dislike admitting that Britain is economically weak, and persist as long as they can with the fiction that we are an economically powerful country suffering temporary adversity. There is still, in their minds, the old correlation between military power and importance and standing in the world.

The second main reason is that most such negotiations in NATO obviously involve a strong military influence. And the British military could hardly be expected to put much weight behind the presentation of a case which would lead to a diminution of their power and influence.

Political Consequences

Much of the objection to reducing defence expenditure is derived from unthinking political dogma, but it is certain that a reduction of the order envisaged in this paper would have serious political repercussions throughout NATO as well as at home.

Apart from domestic considerations, which are very important and form the bulk of this paper's content, the reaction of our NATO allies is the major factor which has so far dominated discussion of this subject. Two main arguments are advanced: first, that defence cuts would weaken the confidence and cohesion of the NATO countries; secondly, that a cut in the British NATO contribution would alter the balance of power within NATO, and this would have undesirable international repercussions.

One particular problem would arise if the Federal Republic of Germany, which has Europe's strongest economy, should decide to follow the logic of the burden-sharing argument and increase her level of military spending. Besides the fact that such a move would alarm the USSR out of all proportion to its intent or real strategic significance, it could also have internal repercussions in that it might provide a justification for increased authoritarianism in German society. As internationalists, the Labour Party shares this concern and recognizes its relevance for ourselves. However, we do not believe that reductions in British military spending will have a decisive effect one way or the other.

The concern about possible shifts in the balance of power within NATO is a valid one, but as it is presented in some quarters it makes it appear that we should be aiming to keep pace with our friends rather than our enemies. This is an element in the fallacy that we can compensate for our economic weakness by military strength. It is, in any case, worth questioning whether the pursuit of status is a particularly worthwhile objective, and whether it justifies the expenditure of a high proportion of our resources. One might as strongly argue that status will not result from hankering after past and discredited glories, and is probably more a function of economic than of military strength.

Conclusion

Let us suppose that the United Kingdom informed its NATO allies that, over the next five years, it was intending to bring down its share of national product devoted to defence to match their average figure. Would the strategic and political consequences be so damaging as to outweigh the economic benefits? The evidence clearly points to the answer: no. This is not a plea for other European countries to make good the deficit caused by a British reduction. On the contrary, it must be stressed that the Labour Party would not see this as a desirable outcome since it views defence cuts as part of a process towards the lessening of military tension. While the current military balance in world affairs is dominated by the actions of the super-powers, it seems unfortunate for the European nations to be dragged into an arms race, the outcome (and indeed direction) of which is entirely beyond their control. Should the super-powers wish to pursue these dangerous policies, they must be firmly told that Europe will not be helping to finance their extravagance.

The desirable political and strategic approach to defence cuts is therefore that they should contribute to multilateral disarmament at best, or at least make way for a more rational assessment of the military threat and ensure the maintenance of the necessary strategic posture at a more realistic cost. In European terms, this would involve the deployment of new military technology as well as specialization among the allies to rationalize the defence effort. There is no suggestion of disarming Britain, and we certainly hope that the debate on these proposals will recognize that we are proposing to defend ourselves in a more rational way, at a more appropriate cost. On the basis of our work, we believe this to be eminently possible as well as desirable.

Notes and References
1. Based on 1976 expenditure figures given in the *Military Balance, 1976–77*, which shows a total of £159,975 million for the military expenditure of all NATO countries.
2. Debate on the Defence Estimates 1977, Cmnd 6735; *Hansard*, 22 March 1977, col. 1113.
3. *Hansard*, 28 March 1977, cols. 58–9.
4. Statement on the Defence Estimates 1977, Cmnd 6735, February 1977, p. 2.
5. This is rather a complex question. For further discussion, see, e.g., Vernon Aspaturian, *Process and Power in Soviet Foreign Policy*, Little Brown, New York, 1971; and M. Schwartz, *The Foreign Policy of the USSR: Domestic Factors*, Dickenson Publishing, New York, 1975, Ch. 6.
6. Robert Kaiser in the *Guardian*, 14 March 1977.
7. Alexander R. Vershbow, 'The Cruise Missile: The End of Arms Control', *Foreign Affairs*, No. 55 (i), October 1976, p. 146.
8. ibid., p. 135.
9. R. G. Horn, 'Détente Myths and Soviet Foreign Policy', in Potichnyj, P. J., and Shapiro, J. P. (eds.), *From Cold War to Détente*, p. 104. See also Schwartz, *The Foreign Policy of the*

USSR, pp. 146, 148–9, 154–6; and Levgold, R., 'The Soviet Union and Western Europe', in W. E. Griffith (ed.), *The Soviet Empire, Expansion and Détente*, Lemington Books, New York, 1976, pp. 230–31.

10. For fuller discussion of Soviet motives in pursuing détente policies, see Levgold, R., 'The Soviet Union and Western Europe', in Griffith (ed.), *The Soviet Empire*, pp. 234–6, 243–4; and G. A. Flynn, 'The Content of European Détente', *Orbis*, vol. 20, No. 2, Summer 1976.

11. See J. S. Berliner and F. D. Halzman, 'The Soviet Economy: Domestic and International Issues', in Griffith (ed.), *The Soviet Empire*.

12. *The Military Balance 1976/77*, IISS, London, 1976.

13. Adam B. Ulam, *Expansion and Co-Existence*, Praeger Publishers, New York, 1974, p. 771.

14. Thomas W. Wolfe, 'Military Power and Soviet Policy', in Griffith (ed.), *The Soviet Empire*, p. 150. See also Ulan, *Expansion and Co-Existence*, p. 678.

15. Robert S. McNamara, *The Essence of Security*, Hodder & Stoughton, London, 1968.

16. Michael McGuire, 'Soviet Naval Capabilities and Intentions', paper presented to the RUSL Conference on the Soviet Union in Europe and the Far East, Milford-on-Sea, 1970.

17. Michael Klare, 'Super-power Rivalry at Sea', in *Foreign Policy*, Winter 1975–6.

18. Statement on the Defence Estimates 1976, Cmnd 6432, ch. 1, para. 20.

19. Henry Stanhope in *The Times*, 31 May 1977, gives the NATO figure; and the Warsaw Pact figure is quoted from Professor William Kaufmann, a Pentagon consultant analyst from MIT.

20. All figures from *The Military Balance 1976/77*, p. 99.

21. Alan C. Enthoven, *Review of a System Analysis Evaluation of NATO v Warsaw Pact Conventional forces*, 90th Congress Report of the Special Sub-Committee on the National Defense Posture of the Committee on Armed Services, US House of Representatives.

22. See Appendix XI: Dan Smith, 'The Political and Strategic Implications of Reduced Defence Programmes'.

23. 'Study Insists NATO Can Defend Itself', *Washington Post*, 7 June 1973.

24. See *The Military Balance*, p. 110; and *SIPRI Yearbook 1976*, p. 151.

25. Les Aspin, 'How to Look at the Soviet–American Balance', *Foreign Policy*, No. 22, Spring 1976.

26. *The Military Balance*, p. 106 (figures refer to mid 1976).

27. Quoted in 'Planning for the Day the Yanks Go Home', *Guardian*, 17 March 1977.

28. *The Military Balance*, p. 103.

29. *Guardian*, 17 March 1977.

30. Smith, Appendix XI.

31. A. Wohlstetter, *Foreign Policy*, No. 25, Winter 1976–7.

32. The basis of this discussion is to be found in Appendix V: David Greenwood, 'Defence Programme Options 1980–81'. It should be

noted that these suggestions were first made in 1975 and a few have been overtaken by events; as an illustrative exercise, however, it remains valid.

33. See Annual Defense Department Report FY 1977 (US, DoD) Sec. III/A, p. 99; and Sec. III/D/1, p. 106.
34. The case for the retention of Polaris is argued in Appendix VI: Paul Cockle, 'Note on the Budget Approach and a Programme Option Which Retains the UK Nuclear Strategic Forces'.
35. See Appendix XI for a fuller discussion of the implications of scrapping Polaris.
36. See Appendix XI for a fuller discussion of naval roles and alternatives to present planning.
37. Calculations based on *The Military Balance 1976/77*, pp. 97–105.
38. The scope of reorganization is discussed in Appendix XI. Appendix XI.
39. Steven Canby: *The Alliance and Europe, Part IV: Military Doctrine and Technology*, Adelphi Paper No. 109 (London, IISS) 1974/5, p. 24.
40. For a fuller discussion of these points, see Appendix XI.
41. See William D. White, *US Tactical Air Power* (Washington DC, Brookings Institution), 1974, for a discussion of the problems of multi-role aircraft.
42. See Appendix XI for a more detailed discussion.
43. *A System of International Comparisons of Gross Product and Purchasing Power*, UN, World Bank, and University of Pennsylvania. The 1970 comparisons are brought up to date by the movements of real GNP, 1970 to 1976.
44. Note that if the comparisons were made at current exchange rates, instead of at purchasing-power parities, the gap between income per head in this country and in France and Germany would be very much wider.

5

CREATING NEW JOBS

Introduction

If a worker is faced with the choice of producing armaments or joining the dole queue, quite naturally he will opt for producing armaments. He would also take this option if he were offered an alternative job which he regarded as being of lower status, or one which required him to move to another part of the country. That he believes this to be the only choice is understandable. There has been no systematic attempt by the Government to identify an 'alternative future', and there has been no methodical investigation of the employment consequences of a lower defence effort. As a result, defence cuts are always associated with redundancy, and working people know exactly what this means. Redundancy highlights the powerlessness of workers, and demonstrates how influences wholly outside their control can completely disrupt their lives, sense of security and expectations. When, for example, the Government decided to cancel the Blue Water guided missile project in 1962, half of those made redundant were forced to accept new jobs which paid less. Six per cent of them were dismissed without the prospect of another job. No magic market mechanism is going to give the redundant armaments worker a new job as of right.

At the same time, it must be remembered that defence expenditure is not designed to maintain employment. If it were, there would be no problem, for it would be cheaper to continue the payment of salaries to workers in the industry and stop other

77

expenditure on arms. It seems strange that those who advance the erroneous proposition that the defence budget is necessary to maintain employment tend to be the same as those who are calling for public expenditure cuts so as to release resources for industrial expansion. Yet more resources and fewer employees are tied up in defence than in any other public sectors. The freeing of resources for other purposes should be seen as an asset rather than as a potential unemployment statistic and liability.

Our argument is that it will be possible over not too long a period to release some of the resources at present tied up in the arms programme for more socially and economically useful production, and without causing unemployment or more than a small minority of workers to change their place of work. Not only is this transformation possible, but it is necessary if we are to restructure and regenerate the British economy. If we do not divert capital formation into the non-military sector, and if we do not redeploy defence workers into productive work, the anticipated upturn in the economy will be retarded, just as it was in 1951 and 1973. In particular, the shortage of skilled workers outside the defence sector is liable to hinder growth itself. Moreover, the ability to convert the economy to civilian work may itself be a precondition for a Government to consider peace or disarmament proposals on their own merits.[1]

In the present chapter we demonstrate the possibilities for conversion in the defence industries and show what has actually been achieved in comparable circumstances. Alternatives to the wasteful policy of maintaining a high level of expenditure do exist; the problem of their implementation is one of planning and organization. There is need for planning at a national level, since the choice of appropriate products must be co-ordinated with government priorities in such diverse fields as health, agriculture, transport, energy and manufacturing generally. And there is a need for reorganization at a local level, since the current structure of military institutions, particularly the defence companies, is geared up to military-oriented innovation and tends to preclude domestic civilian investment.

Two terms are used here which should be understood separately. *Conversion* refers to the process by which part of our military industrial capacity would move into a different field of manufacture – a once and for all change. *Diversification* implies a widening of the base of activity – alternating military and non-military work for unconverted capacity.

The Effect of the Proposed Cuts

The money tied up in the defence effort represents resources – industrial capacity, human skills and manual labour. Just under a million people are directly employed in the defence sector. A third of a million servicemen and women are backed by the same number of civil servants. In Chapter 2, we saw that some 200,000 are employed on armaments work for the Ministry of Defence, and about 75,000 on export work; that a further 350,000 are indirectly involved, to some degree, on armaments work.[2]

What then would be the likely consequences of (a) the cut of approximately £1,800 million from the defence budget which would be required by equalizing defence/GNP proportions by the early 1980s, or (b) the reduction of approximately £1,300 million for which precise programme options have been identified in Chapter 2 (pp. 26–30)? A detailed analysis for the smaller reduction suggests that, if effected over a five-year period, the options developed in Chapter 2 would entail an actual release of manpower as shown in Table 12.

TABLE 12.

	Servicemen	MoD civilians	Contractors' employees	Total
Option 1	55,000	37,500	37,500	130,000
Option 2	32,500	27,500	55,000	115,000
Option 3	52,500	37,500	45,000	135,000

SOURCE: See Appendix XII (revised figures in postscript).

Allowing for the multiplier effect, one might double these numbers so that over a five-year period around 50,000 jobs would be lost each year in the defence sector. This is not a trivial adjustment problem, though the number itself is very small indeed when compared with the six million who voluntarily quit their jobs each year to start a new job or retire, or with the two and a half million who simply change jobs. Frank Blackaby[3] has estimated that there are about 180,000 jobs changed each year in the defence sector alone, so the overall number of jobs reduced in the defence sector would not be overwhelming, though the impact would, of course, depend on whereabouts in the country those jobs were located.

79

Contrary to popular belief, defence contracts are not placed predominantly in regions of high unemployment. In fact, whichever option for cutbacks is taken, in the absence of an alternative employment strategy the region which would suffer most would be South-East England in terms of both displaced servicemen and civilians. The South-East has the lowest average unemployment rate, and yet, with 30 per cent of the population, some 40 per cent of defence contracts are placed in this region. By contrast, Wales, with a relatively high rate of unemployment and 5 per cent of the British population, receives less than 3 per cent of defence contracts.[4] This illustrates how the aggregate problem of conversion is not one that would fall disproportionately on those regions least able to cope.

This is merely to put the matter in perspective: the Labour Party does not for a moment deny the extent of the problem within localities. We fully recognize that defence work may, within a region, be concentrated very heavily in a small number of firms and localities; and that a whole town may at present be entirely dependent on the defence industry. These facts clearly underline the need for effective and detailed planning. Much work must be done to ensure a smooth transition. But no one can seriously suggest that land, equipment, labour and skills should be committed to military purposes solely on the grounds that transitional measures would be troublesome.

Learning from Experience

In an exercise of this kind we must be guided by experience. Britain's own previous experience of coping with cutbacks – the successes as well as the failures – is relevant, as is the experience of other countries. In 1945 the Labour Government redeployed nine million people within twelve months. No one suggested that the war should continue to keep people in employment. Similarly, the experience of the railways, the docks, the cotton industry and the mining industry in the post-war period indicates that large reductions in employment in given sectors can be achieved without large-scale unemployment.

In the immediate post-war period, when the main problem was less people than materials, particularly enormous stockpiles of sheet metal, aircraft companies manufactured a wide range of production in such fields as construction and civil engineering, household and office equipment. Shorts, for example, became the largest producer of milk cans in Europe. De Havilland's adapted their vibration test equipment to remove bubbles from milk chocolate. More important than individual examples, however, was the spread of skills and techniques to other industries. Particularly significant from this point of view were high-strength aviation plastics, kinetic heating, heat-resistant materials, light alloys, radar, titanium, glass fabrics, hydraulics and servo-mechanisms. British Rail, notably its establishment at Derby, have made use of design talent from the military aircraft sector, and this has been of particular importance in the development of new rail technology, particularly the high-speed train. English Electric, before it was merged with General Electric, used aero-dynamicists in the development of steam turbines. The civil engineering sector of Hawker Siddeley, best known for the manufacture of diesel engines, has benefited from the transfer of engineers from the military side of the group. (Further examples of conversion in the Naval Dockyards are to be found in Appendix XV.) But while the post-war period demonstrated the potential for transferring production away from military supplies, it also demonstrated the problems which arise when there is an early reversion to military production. For this reason, among others, some of the examples given above proved not particularly successful. Their significance lies in the tangible experience of the potential for converting the arms industries.

Even more information on industrial conversion has been published in the United States, where the scale of the problem is much greater.[5] One significant initiative has been in the field of 'Community Planning'. To help communities overcome the consequences of military cutbacks, the American Department of Defense established an Office of Economic Adjustment (OEA). In each locality subject to a defence cutback, the OEA has been instrumental in establishing the participation of all concerned in planning for conversion. Each community has naturally taken a different stance, but they have all evolved a development strategy. This strategy has consisted of the following six elements:

1. Identification of community assets: plant, land, equipment, people.
2. Market survey, demand forecasting, consumption patterns.
3. Identification of new products.
4. Consideration of constraints, e.g. transportation.
5. Overcoming of constraints, e.g. road-building.
6. Conversion of defence installations.

Local communities have been encouraged by the Defense

Department (through the OEA) to use their knowledge to plan for a smooth transition in an environment which, it should be remembered, is particularly unsympathetic to centralized planning, and with little government aid. As military bases have closed they have been converted, and in some cases where bases have been contracted rather than totally closed, sharing arrangements have been negotiated. For example, Topeka air base in Kansas is now open for both civil and military air transport. Of some forty-six recently converted defence installations, the new uses include industry (in 40 cases), education (33 cases), aviation (27 cases), recreation (25 cases), housing (21 cases), commerce (13 cases), and agriculture (9 cases). A cutback in military activity which was at first viewed as a threat became, thanks to community planning, a challenge and an opportunity. The chief advantage found by the OEA was that a community generally chose prosperity. Several small employers tended to replace one large employer, so giving the area a greater sense of stability. As the OEA said in its 1975 Report: 'The imagined disasters that a base closing portends can actually become catalysts for community improvements never before thought possible.'[6]

These American findings are, for Britain, particularly relevant in the Preston area of Lancashire. Preston very much depends upon work at the BAC factory (where MRCA will be assembled) for its local prosperity. Defence cuts without conversion, or a de-emphasis on military aircraft, could hit Preston hard. However, near Preston, the Central Lancashire Development Corporation is in the process of a new town development which includes industrial development. This will provide the opportunity needed to diversify the basis of Preston's local economy and inject greater stability. Equally, reductions in defence work could release the skilled workforce necessary for industrial development, which could in turn contribute to both local prosperity and revitalizing British industry.

It may be argued that the American experience is not in general especially relevant to Britain since conversion was taking place there in the context of a more dynamic economy, better able to absorb surplus capacity. Yet the fact is that on a long-term basis economic growth rates in the United States and Britain are very similar, apart from the level of unemployment being much higher in America.

One final example of previous experience gives an indication. During the four years 1953–7, the Conservatives cut the defence budget by one third. They did this without any great disruption. In 1953, unemployment stood at 1·5 per cent; in 1957 at 1·4 per cent. In terms of 1976 prices, the Tories cut £1,650 million off the defence budget over four years. Thus, not only can it be done, it has been done.

The Need for Planning

Converting military industrial capacity cannot be left to chance. The measures needed to ensure the smooth transition of resources from military to non-military production are basically the same as those required to solve the economic crisis.

There is no question of leaving the task to market forces or making free handouts to industry. The approach put forward in this study is centred on the need to produce socially useful and necessary products. We know, from bitter experience of the performance of British industry over thirty years, that these products will not emerge without strong planning and control of the process. We must also be aware that the experience and habits of management in military industry will in many ways be unsuited to non-military production; the conditions of military industry are very different from those of civil industries, reflecting different objectives. This aspect is looked at further at a later stage in this chapter. Obviously industrial conversion is not a simple matter of transferring production from the military to the civil sphere since there are often profound problems of over-capacity in certain areas of civil production. On the contrary, the transfer of production should be directed to areas of industry where there are (a) gaps in existing capacity, (b) export demand and (c) the possibility of providing import substitution. Not all alternatives to military production are necessarily desirable, and those likely to increase unemployment are especially to be avoided.

The right approach must therefore be a series of obligatory planning agreements, accompanied by energetic public investment and participation in profitable manufacture. We must, however, be careful to distinguish two types of 'profitability'. The first type is the one with which we are all familiar: returns should be greater than investment. The second type could be described as 'social profitability': the gain to society of producing, for example, well-made medical equipment to improve the NHS, or cheap and effective methods of energy generation. This would introduce a new criterion of 'profitability' into the economy. Such manufacturers, where there would be significant public investment and control if not full public ownership, should not

necessarily be expected to perform 'profitably' by showing sur-
pluses in their accounts since society would be profiting from
their products. It is also important to ensure that the way in
which the defence industries are to be run down should not
determine priorities in public spending. In other words, the
existence of new industrial capacity should not of itself influence
priorities for the choice of products to be purchased by the public
sector. As the Government is likely to be the most important
customer for many of these products, it will be in a position to
play a leading role in planning, both by defining its requirement
and by ensuring the stability of the market for the new products.

A party and a Government already committed to planning
the general direction of the economy, and to controlling important sectors, should find nothing especially daunting in the
task of planning to convert the defence sector. The opportunities
provided by conversion can, with effective and imaginative
planning, take our aspirations for society a further stage towards
achievement.

Planning will be necessary at both local and national level.
The Government's main role would be to co-ordinate local plans.
It would need to supply financial assistance to the localities concerned, and to industries establishing themselves. Aid to those
industries may also need to include selective import controls for a
period to allow new products to establish themselves on the market. Finally, the Government will need to keep an eye on the
whole process – a kind of 'watchdog' role.

The details of planning must be expected to emerge at local
level. As noted below, the best ideas for alternative products have
emerged from the work-forces involved, including both development and production staffs. It is they who best know what other
uses exist for their plant, skills and ingenuity. It is they who can
best form the creative basis of conversion planning. Without
their input to the planning process by way of a system of planning
agreements, we cannot expect the opportunities which present
themselves to be fully utilized.

It is not only the workforce of affected plants that must be
involved at a local level. The wider local communities also have a
stake in the conversion process. Through trade councils, community organizations and local authorities, they must also have
a real say in the planning. Knowledge of the facilities available
in the area, and of the constraints there may be upon the introduction of certain industries, is an equally important ingredient
of proper planning. Many of the most imaginative and practical

suggestions for conversion have come from the shop floor. In one case, at the BAC factories in Preston, the joint shop stewards have even offered to forgo 1 per cent of a proposed wage claim if the firm would devote the amount saved (£300,000 per annum) to research and development into converting production to civil products.[7]

Decentralization is entirely consistent with a general planning approach. Indeed, widening participation in the planning stage should inject a needed urgency, creativeness and concern for the interests of those affected in the process, as well as avoiding the dangers of bureaucratization. We must now, however, examine two elements in such a plan which are of particular importance. One concerns planning for the conversion of the product, the other planning for the conversion of occupations.

Production Conversion

The objective is to plan for conversion so that workers no longer make armaments which are no longer wanted by society. It would be absurd if such workers should now commence to make some other equally useless product. Any new product which is to be produced by former armaments workers must be one that is needed, and the first stage in a product conversion plan must be the 'product search'. Long before it announces a particular defence cutback, the Government should require the contractor involved to establish a joint management–union committee to evaluate the possibilities for alternative products. Rather than dismissing the firm – and the workers – with a cancellation fee, it should subsidize the market research. The joint committee will need to consider all the distribution outlets, and to negotiate licences and patents. As we shall see, workers in the armaments industries are already developing new technologies in anticipation of possible cuts. Their ideas are ones which would be economically and socially useful, improve Britain's competitive position and reverse the trend towards boring and dehumanizing work. Yet only proper planning can successfully bring about the conversion of 'threats' to 'opportunities'.

Two alternative routes for product conversion are distinguishable. One is the commercial route: to improve the efficiency of current product lines. For example, one of our tasks is to revitalize Britain's existing industries, from motor-cycles to textiles, from electronics to machine tools. The capital resources released from defence could be invested to modernize those industries which are heavily under attack from foreign competitors. We

85

have seen that the armament sector is also the capital goods sector, and that a reconversion of armaments production to the production of capital goods could therefore make an important contribution towards progress in manufacturing. Our existing problems are not the result of a lack of demand for the products but of a lack of efficiency in the industries concerned.

It should nevertheless be recognized that, in a deteriorating international economic climate, the cost of improving the efficiency of certain commercial product lines, such as merchant shipbuilding, may prove prohibitive. Furthermore, any gains made in Britain's competitiveness will be at the expense of workers elsewhere. It might therefore be more fruitful to concentrate on the second alternative for product conversion: the search for new products which satisfy social needs not currently being filled by either ourselves or imports. (See pp. 88–96, for a list of examples.) In the first instance, some of these would be commercially viable in that they would be purchased by private customers, for example, power-packs for cars to reduce fuel consumption and polluting emissions, heat pumps for private homes, and so forth. For others, the Government would be the main customer. Such social expenditure would cost the Government no more, and probably much less, than current expenditure on the dole or on defence. Nor is there any reason to suppose it would reduce foreign exchange earnings: as we have seen, the armament sector is rather inefficient at exporting compared with civilian sectors in the same industry, while there would be some saving of military costs. There would also need to be changes in government policy in other areas, since many of the suggestions made may run counter to current government priorities. For example, suggestions for transport place more emphasis on railways and canals than on roads, while the energy projects aim to provide alternatives to oil, coal and nuclear energy.

In summary, it may be said that proper planning can eliminate the problems which concern the demand for the new products. In the words of a United Nations report: 'There are so many competing claims for usefully employing the resources released by disarmament that the real problem is to establish a scale of priorities.'[8]

Occupational Conversion
We have argued that the market would not pose insurmountable problems to a conversion of production. But what of the workers themselves? There is a need for the Manpower Services Com-

86

mission to undertake detailed 'manpower audits' at each locality where conversion is planned. The information needed will cover the types of skills possessed by the workers, their turnover levels, the travel-to-work catchment areas and so on. Some retraining or upgrading of skill levels might be desirable, but it is probable that this would be smaller than is generally assumed. On the other hand, planning is necessary, not only to avoid unemployment, but also to avoid bottlenecks in the form of shortages of skilled workers. It might be possible to de-skill some of the work, but it would be far better to upgrade the level of skills. Let us consider some of the occupational groups which would be involved.

The production occupations would cause little problem. In the 1960s in California, where there is a high concentration of military aerospace production, a detailed examination was carried out by the State Department of Employment on 127 production occupations.[9] Of these, twenty-eight were of the 'basic' craft-types, for example, 'carpenter', 'plumber' and so on. A further ninety-three could be matched to one or more non-military production occupations. Only six occupational groups were found to require retraining. Similar conclusions were reached by US Federal Government Survey.[10] In Britain, research has produced comparable results in relation to, for example, the Clyde submarine base[11] and the Vickers shipyard at Barrow-in-Furness.[12]

Civil servants – the administrators – would probably constitute the hardest conversion challenge because of their lack of outside experience. But the task would not be impossible, and with suitable training they could develop management skills suitable for the new industries. Among the ranks of existing civil servants are the Defence Sales Organization export salesmen. The release of these skills would be a boon to our manufacturing industry, which is very short of competent export salesmen.

Conversion also demands a change of attitudes. Experience has taught military scientists that the main target is not cost-effectiveness. We certainly would not want to see the cost of, for example, medical equipment spiralling upwards through unnecessary extra sophistication for marginal or illusory benefits.

Many administrators would be sure to find posts in the public programmes that would be expanded after arms cuts, and the management sectors of converted industries could be expected to absorb many. As with occupational conversion in general, this should not be left to chance, and where different management

87

techniques are appropriate, retraining should be made available, possibly for periods of around six months.

Numerous skills are available in the lower ranks of the armed forces, in civil and mechanical engineering, communications, electronics and so on. Some of these skills are directly applicable to civilian employment, while others would provide a sound basis on which to build a short period of retraining. Given the likelihood that arms cuts would create more jobs than are provided at present, it should be possible to utilize these skills in converted industry to everybody's advantage. Many other servicemen, however, will not have these skills, and will need to start in retraining almost from scratch. Adequate provision for this should be guaranteed, and could most valuably include opportunities for these servicemen to enter apprenticeships.

A reduction in recruitment levels would be sufficient to overcome the problem caused by a rundown in servicemen. Yet the matter does not end there. It would also be necessary to consider the working-class youth in the depressed areas who traditionally join the services. Once again, the solution to the problem is the same as the solution to the present crisis: a vigorous regional policy as part of an overall strategy of industrial and social regeneration.

Case-studies in Alternative Employment Possibilities
If we are to overcome the natural hostility of defence workers to plans for conversion we must be more than theoretical. The alternatives must be concrete and practical. There is no specific blueprint, but the following pages show that practical planning for conversion is possible. It is up to the Government to provide the facilities and the general policy which can translate the possibilities outlined into practical reality for the workers in the industries concerned.[13]

(a) Alternatives in the Aerospace Industry
The major military aerospace project for Britain at present – and for Italy and Germany – is the development of the multi-role combat aircraft (MRCA), the Tornado. Although only 10 per cent of British aerospace workers are at present engaged on Tornado, a major project like this generates other associated projects.

Tornado is an unusually expensive aircraft. The latest government estimate puts the unit production cost (in 1977/8 Estimates

88

Prices) at £6·3 million for the IDS (Interceptor or 'common' variant), of which 220 copies will be produced, and £7·72 million for the ADV (Air Defence Variant), of which 165 copies are expected to be produced.[14] For the study group it has been calculated, using a widely accepted convention, that the total unit cost, including development and maintenance, will be £16·7 million for the IDS and £20·3 million for the ADV – a total cost for the whole project of £7,000 million in the same prices. The high cost is caused by the multiplicity of roles which the aircraft is expected to perform; it will thus, by definition, have many wasted characteristics. It is being built as an all-weather, long-range aircraft with a large weapon load, accurate weapon delivery, manoeuvrability, rapid acceleration and climb, and subsonic, short take-off and landing capabilities. The Tornado is a classic example of tremendous sophistication providing over-specialization on the one hand and under-utilization on the other.

While it is questionable whether it would be feasible to scrap the Tornado project, it is worth looking at the nature of the resources devoted to its production, mainly to demonstrate the skills and potential in the aerospace industry as well as to caution against embarking on similar projects in the future. Some 17,000 workers are at present directly and indirectly involved in Tornado. This is expected to rise to a maximum of 36,000.[15] Half of these workers are employed by BAC in Lancashire and Rolls-Royce in Bristol. The others are employed by such firms as GEC Marconi-Elliott, Lucas Aerospace, Dunlop, Decca, Ferranti and Plessey. This study's task is therefore to consider what alternative work could be found for these people in the event of the project's cancellation. But we might equally consider their plight once Tornado production has passed its peak, for it is questionable whether Britain could afford a comparable successor. Even without defence cuts, there is an urgent need to consider diversification possibilities simply to give greater stability and security to an industry which has serious structural problems. Two measures may be expected to assist in this process: one is the nationalization of the aircraft industry, the other is a measure of industrial democracy. Together these will help to facilitate effective planning for conversion.

(b) The Airframe Industry

Tired of the fluctuations in work levels, and the hiring and firing that go with it, the BAC Shop Stewards Combine Committee has advanced a claim for 'Job Protection Agreements'. In this they are seeking alternative work during the troughs in military aerospace production, like those which occur during the gaps between the peaks in Jaguar and Tornado production. However, there are many flaws in the concept of 'Job Protection Agreements', and these have been highlighted in a paper written by Peter Ward, a BAC Preston Shop Steward, which is now before the Combine Committee and entitled 'Alternatives to Arms Production'.[16]

The problem of merely filling in with alteratives during a lull in military production is this: in a competitive market, once one has put a foot in the door with an alternative product, a continuous effort is needed to keep it there. It is no good making machine tools for a few months and stopping when more military work comes along. There is, first, a need to establish the level of military aircraft development and what production capacity will be compatible with our economic capacity. Secondly, the remaining aircraft capacity should be permanently converted. Thirdly, the first part should be diversified. This will be a major planning risk, but the alternative is the continuation of present threats of redundancy, waste of resources and the surplus capacity which provides the impetus for the weapons procurement policy.

Many options are available for diversification. As McDonagh and Zimmerman comment: 'The primary resource of the [airframe] industry is its ability to design, develop and manufacture new and advanced products.'[17] Diversification has been suggested in such new areas (where there is no harsh market competition) as barrage schemes, nuclear material disposal schemes, solar-panel generators, rolling stock and prefabricated parts for the construction industry.

(c) *Aero-engines*

The main aero-engine manufacturer, Rolls-Royce, does, of course, already diversify its operations between military and civil aircraft production. In particular, Rolls-Royce is internationally competitive in the civil aviation field. Further diversification options are possible. The company has found a market for adaptations of engines for civil non-aerospace use. Processing plants, which have long lead times, could be built using BAC infrastructure and Rolls-Royce engines. These would make an ideal diversification option. Rolls-Royce workers – and managers – would be well advised to consider partial conversion in addition. This would mean that military production would continue, but that there could be civil alternatives. The American competitor,

Pratt & Whitney, has already converted some of its capacity to manufacturing machine tools.

(d) *The Equipment Suppliers – Lucas Aerospace*

The most celebrated proposals for alternative production are those which have been drawn up by the Lucas Aerospace workers. The Shop Stewards Combine Committee, faced with a permanent threat of redundancies, decided to put forward their own corporate plan which would, if implemented, provide their members with work on socially useful products.

> The object of the Corporate Plan [say its authors] is twofold. Firstly, to protect our members' right to work by proposing a range of alternative products on which they could become engaged in the event of further cutbacks in the aerospace industry. Secondly, to ensure that among the alternative products proposed are a number which would be socially useful to the community at large.[18]

Lucas Aerospace employs some 13,000 highly skilled design and manual staffs in thirteen sites in Britain. It is the largest manufacturer of electrical generating systems in Europe, and also produces gas-turbine engine starting and control systems, power units, instruments, medical equipment and so on. However, a large part of its business is connected with military aircraft projects, including the Tornado. The Combine Committee thought that there would be no point in organizing 'sit-ins' to maintain the production of something that nobody wanted. They decided therefore to seek ideas for alternative products from trade union headquarters and from academics. The result was disappointing, and the shop stewards turned instead to their own workforce, distributing questionnaires to all the workers. As a result, some 150 designs for alternative products were submitted to the Combine Committee. All the products aimed at using rather than displacing people; all involved the adaptation of existing design techniques and experience. The Corporate Plan is, consequently, not an aspiration or a moral assertion. It is a series of concrete proposals which have been widely acclaimed in the specialist press.[19] Prototypes for a whole series of socially useful products are already in existence, and six large volumes of technical data have been collected.

The alternative products include power packs and microprocessors which would assist the development of low-energy housing, telecheiric machines for use in dangerous environments, and submersibles for exploring the ocean bed. Alternative products which would make transport more efficient, safer and less of an environmental hazard include battery cars which could be recharged by a diesel or petrol hybrid power pack (thus overcoming the present problem with such cars), braking systems which would adapt the eddy-current dynamometer technology to existing coach retarders, and the hybrid road/rail vehicle featured on the television programme, *Tomorrow's World*. The prototype of this is being considered for use by the Highlands and Islands Development Board; with its gradient ability of 1 : 6, the hybrid vehicle would be very cheap to run, particularly when compared with the cost of constructing conventional low-gradient railways. The plan also proposes a whole range of alternative energy-producing equipment. In the field of medical equipment, there are three products listed: first are kidney machines, which are already manufactured by both Lucas and Vickers. A second product which the workers want to manufacture is the 'hobcart'. This was originally designed and built by apprentices at Lucas's Wolverhampton factory for the benefit of children suffering from spina bifida. Finally, the aerospace workers would like to develop aids for blind people. Aerospace technology could easily be adapted and applied to assist those who have no sight, using exactly the same principle as the 'blind landing system' in the Tornado.[20]

Lucas stewards envisage a phased transition from military to civilian work. Some of the products could be manufactured immediately, while others are longer term. The object would be initially to arrest the contraction of the industry, and then to reverse it gradually as diversification increases. Lucas would be an ideal company for a tripartite planning agreement. Thus, the local initiatives could be co-ordinated and assisted, maximizing the benefits to society as a whole.

The management reply to the Combine Committee was unfortunately predictable. As the *Engineer* reported:

Management based its reply on a reaffirmation of its established business strategy. In so doing it paid no regard to the damage to personnel morale inflicted on highly qualified senior engineers, technologists and shopfloor engineering workers.[21]

The initiative now lies with the Government.

(e) *The Shipbuilding Industry*

In considering shipbuilding, we are conscious of the way in which entire localities have come to be dependent on particular naval orders. For example, about 40 per cent of the male employees in Barrow-in-Furness[22] are employed by Vickers, and about one fifth of Vickers's shipbuilding and engineering capacity in Barrow is taken up with the design, development and production of a large aircraft-carrying warship known as the 'Anti-Submarine Warfare Cruiser'. The cruiser is likely to cost around £100 million over a period of five years.

Vickers is one of the oldest armaments companies in Britain. After each war it has faced the problem of diversification. The company's experience indicates the technical possibility of conversion. The Barrow shipyard has manufactured such diverse items as cement kilns, sugar-beet crushers and irrigation systems. It also indicates the need for central government control and planning, since Vickers has used profits made in the armament sector to diversify into such fields as office equipment and lithographic plates, often through the acquisition of foreign subsidiaries.

In terms of the equipment and skills which would be released at Barrow by a cutback in defence expenditure, and considering such factors as the marine experience of the workers and the poor road and rail access, a study of the available resources points in the direction of alternative production being of a sea-based nature. Shipbuilding skills and facilities are commensurate with any kind of large-scale and relatively labour-intensive construction and assembly activities which involve heavy metal fabrication and materials handling, and complex logistic problems of supply, storage and scheduling. A study commissioned by the US Government identified fifty-five conventional product ranges into which shipbuilding could be converted, and demonstrated that, over a three-year period, a third of total US naval building capacity could be converted by capturing 10 per cent of the annual *growth* of the market for these products.[23]

The prospects for merchant shipbuilding are poor because of the huge over-capacity in world shipbuilding which is forecast. But there do seem to be opportunities in the new technologies now being developed to make use of the sea and the sea-bed. A high proportion of designers and electricians employed at a naval shipyard could prove a positive asset in such fields as marine agriculture and mining, oil drilling, marine-based energy sources and new forms of marine transport. Already, Vickers Offshore Engineering, based in Barrow, is in the forefront of development and submersibles. Other products which have been suggested include wave-power generators, fish-farming tanks, ocean-going tub-barge container ships and the Morecambe Bay barrage system (for tidal power).

The point has been made earlier that the problem of conversion to socially useful production is not technical, but one of political will. The Vickers Company aggravated the situation by hiving off its non-shipbuilding activities into a separate company to minimize the extent of nationalization in advance of the Aircraft and Shipbuilding Act. This development makes the diversification and conversion of the military shipbuilding activities difficult. In addition, Vickers has already implied that it intends to spend its compensation money from nationalization on its private-enterprise activities abroad. Thus, to cope with the problems of under-investment and conversion, there is a need for active government involvement in this particular area. The idea of leaving industry alone is diametrically opposed to the idea of a planned conversion for socially useful production.

(f) *Alternative Employment in Other Industries*
Industrial sectors which would greatly benefit from a release of resources from military use are mechanical engineering, machine tools, electronics and telecommunications. In Sweden, for example, computers which were initially developed for fast decision-making in complex military situations have been adapted for hospital management. But of more importance than the release of equipment is the release of human skills. A real shortage of skilled workers is hindering the development of vital sections of British industry, including the orderly development of the North Sea oilfields. Some 60 per cent of qualified scientists and engineers in mechanical engineering are at present engaged on military work, and yet this work accounts for less than 30 per cent of the total domestic output. The skills tied up in the military sector are not being used efficiently.

(g) *Alternative Employment at the Clyde Submarine Base*
The Labour Party and the Government have given a Manifesto commitment not to develop a second generation of nuclear warheads.[24] Thus, even without a new cutback in defence spending, there is a need to consider the plight of the Clyde Polaris Submarine Base in Faslane. The base, which generates about 8·5 per cent of the economic activity in West Dunbartonshire, was the subject of an investigation in 1975 by the Scottish Campaign for Nuclear Disarmament, for whom an economic profile

94

of the base and an analysis of the employment (and other) consequences of rundown were prepared by the University of Aberdeen's Defence Studies Unit.

The base provides work for 3,100 servicemen, most of whom are 'posted' to the area, as well as 2,800 civilian support workers and 2,000 indirect workers in the surrounding service industries. The composition of the workforce is as follows (the total of 100 per cent allowing for rounding):

Managerial, scientific, technical	21%
Clerical	19%
Skilled craftsmen	14%
Semi-skilled and unskilled	45%

Some 80 per cent of the skilled craftsmen are mechanical and electrical fitters.

The survey team took this job mix and tried to see what alternative industries would use such a range of skills, and considered a number of options.

The first option was that of gradually closing the base completely, with no alternative employment being created. By the time the base closed, it was estimated, all the servicemen and some 1,000 of the 'posted' civilians would have moved on as a matter of course. Another 500 might be expected to migrate, leaving 3,000 workers to receive unemployment benefit. However, it was felt that even the payment of very high levels of unemployment benefit would be unacceptable since the object of the exercise was to release manpower for useful work rather than the dole queue. A second option involved the migration of workers to the developing Scottish east coast. (This structural change is already occurring; the total population of the Strathclyde region fell by 33,000 between 1971 and 1973.) A third option envisaged the cancellation of Polaris, but the continuation of conventional naval activity at the base. A fourth option involved the creation of new jobs in the same location as the former military base.

This fourth option might be of one major project, or smaller diverse projects, which would use existing resources. The survey team looked at the present job mix and decided that petrochemical work would not 'fit'. Oil platform construction work was considered to be an uneconomic proposition on the west coast of Scotland, since even Marathon found itself with empty order books at the end of 1976. However, two other alternatives seemed viable. One was electrical instrument engineering, and the other the development of submerged oil production systems like those being developed at present in the USA by Exxon. If there is too great a loss of skilled workers in the transitional period, the level of skills of the 45 per cent semi-skilled and unskilled workers in the transitional period could be upgraded by special MSC training courses, or the skilled work itself could be broken down into semi-skilled component and assembly work. This has already occurred on Tees-side, where a shortage of skilled welders has led to the development of friction bolting.

The American experience of 'Community Planning' described earlier in this chapter is clearly relevant in this sort of base conversion.

Conclusion
In this chapter we have advocated the permanent conversion of a large part of the military sector. We have illustrated that it is possible, and that it has been done before, both in the United Kingdom and elsewhere. There are, of course, problems arising from conversion which must be taken very seriously, but these are distinctly soluble. This chapter has shown how the obstacles might be overcome and, indeed, turned into golden opportunities. All that is required is the will to act.

There is something paradoxical about the way in which we devote valuable and highly talented human resources to the manufacture of complex and sophisticated instruments of destruction while so many basic needs remain unrealized. For example, even in an advanced industrial country like Britain, old people suffer from hypothermia and children with chronic diseases are not adequately treated. And yet there are plenty of workers currently unemployed or employed in the defence sector who have the skills, ability and motivation to provide the means of solving these problems.

It is up to the Government to show determination and to start the necessary detailed planning immediately. They should set the pace in the public sector through the National Enterprise Board. Nationalization of the shipbuilding and aerospace industries presents opportunities which should not be missed. It is crucial to protect the right of these industries to diversify their operations, and equally important for this opportunity to be taken up. In the private sector, the pace must be forced through by the vigorous use of planning agreements. In both sectors, the planning process must harness the imagination of the defence workers themselves,

96

through the implementation of our policies for the joint control and public accountability of industry.[25]

Notes and References
1. See Seymour Melman, *The Defence Economy*, Columbia University Press, 1970.
2. *Hansard*, 19 October 1976.
3. Appendix XII: Frank Blackaby, 'Note on the Employment Consequences of a £1,000 million Cut (at 1974 prices) in Military Expenditure over Five Years'.
4. Secretary of State for Defence: Parliamentary Written Answers, *Hansard*, 22 May 1975 and 9 June 1975.
5. See Appendix XVII: Dan Smith, 'Community Planning and Base Conversion', for a further discussion.
6. *Economic Recovery*, Office of Economic Adjustment, Washington DC, 1975, p. 4.
7. The claim is in addition to the 5 per cent annual pay claim; as reported in the *Lancashire Evening Post*, January 1977.
8. 'Economic and Social Consequences of Disarmament', United Nations Department of Economic and Social Affairs, 1962, para. 169.
9. 'The Potential Transfer of Industrial Skills from Defense to Non-Defense Industries', Californian Department of Employment, 1968.
10. Camborn, J. R. and Newton, D, 'Skills Transfers', in *Monthly Labor Review*, US Department of Labor, June 1969.
11. 'Replacing Employment at the Nuclear Bases', Scottish CND, February 1975.
12. Appendix XV: Mary Kaldor, 'Alternative Employment for Naval Shipbuilding Workers: A Case-Study of the Resources Devoted to the Production of the ASW Cruiser'.
13. A list of alternative products for manufacture in the industries no longer making military goods is given in Appendix II.
14. *Hansard*, 9 November 1976, col. 199.
15. See Appendix XVI: Dan Smith, 'Tornado – Cancellation, Conversion and Diversification in the Aerospace Industry', for breakdown.
16. Peter Ward, 'Alternatives to Arms Production', paper presented to Preston North Constituency Labour Party Two-Day School, 2 April 1976.
17. McDonagh, J. J. and Zimmerman, S. M., 'Mobilization for Peace: a Program for Civilian Diversification of the Airframe Industry', unpublished thesis, Columbia University, 1961, p. 181.
18. 'Corporate Plan – a Contingency Strategy as a Positive Alternative to Recession and Redundancies', published by the Lucas Aerospace Combine Shop Stewards Committee, 1976.
19. See, for example, the *New Scientist*, 3 July 1975 and 16 September 1976; *Engineer*, 5 February 1976 and 13 May 1976; *Industrial Management*, July 1976.
20. Further details are available from the Secretary of the Combine Committee: Mr E. Scarbrow, 86 Mellow Lane East, Hayes, Middlesex.

21. *Engineer*, 13 May 1976.
22. The basic research for this section is drawn from Mary Kaldor, Appendix XV, and evidence from the MP for Barrow, Mr Albert Booth.
23. 'Final Report on Industrial Conversion Potential in the Ship-building Industry', Mid-West Research Institute Contract No. ACDA/E, 1966.
24. *Labour Party Manifesto*, October 1974, p. 29.
25. See *Labour's Programme 1976*, pp. 33–6.

6

THE ARMS TRADE

About a quarter of British arms production goes to the export trade.[1] In so doing, it makes this country one of the 'Big Four' arms exporters, probably slightly behind France but considerably behind the two super-powers. Any serious programme for cutting defence expenditure must therefore have implications for the nature and extent of our continuing trade in arms. The two problems are interrelated, and any strategy directed towards the overall reduction of military production must take into account the export dimension. Indeed, the very presence of demand for military hardware abroad, and the existence of industrial capacity to meet this demand, constitutes one of the most frequently cited arguments for maintaining a high level of defence expenditure, which is in turn a concomitant of maintaining a high level of military capacity. If no other reasons existed, the political and moral case against the arms trade ought to be sufficient cause for reducing our arms manufacturing capacity.

The Political Argument

While few would question the wisdom of limiting and controlling the international arms race, there are considerable disagreements about how this could be achieved and to what extent it is desirable. Dr Iklé, Director of the United States Arms Control and Disarmament Agency, has summarized the case for his agency's work succinctly:

The goals of arms control, simply stated, are to prevent war and to reduce the destruction of war if it should occur. Limiting the availability of weapons can lessen the chances of war by promoting a stable balance, and mutual reductions in arms can make wars less destructive. Moreover, in the long run, it is to be hoped, arms control will permit us to lower the economic burden of defence.[2]

There is a consensus of opinion which advocates the ideal solution of a multilateral arms control agreement, possibly operating through the UN. As in the great debate over nuclear disarmament, a division exists between those who believe in a unilateral start and those who are disinclined to accept anything less than a multilateral agreement.

There is without doubt some scope for unilateral action by Britain, to set a principled example as well as to respond to our pressing economic need to reduce the level of arms production. The advent of the Carter Administration in the United States has certainly signalled the start of a major initiative towards arms control. Shortly after President Carter's inauguration, Cyrus Vance, the US Secretary of State, said:

We are reviewing our own arms sales policy because we must know what are its objectives and tailor them accordingly. Secondly, our arms sales should be determined by our foreign policy objectives and not by economic ones. Thirdly, once we have determined our own unilateral policy, we may then move on to the question of international agreements to make the policy effective.[3]

The British Labour Government can hardly do less than respond in kind to the Secretary of State's proposals, even if the US will be playing the leading role in this sphere.

The critics of unilateral action argue that British influence in bringing about an international agreement would be more effective as a major supplier nation than as one which had already played its cards by taking independent steps. It would also, they feel, mean that the supply of arms could then fall into the hands of less responsible exporters. And, they argue, British arms supplies to Yugoslavia, for example, help deter a possible Soviet attack, as, similarly, they deter a Guatemalan attack on Belize.

Whatever the truth of these arguments, they tend to ignore the basic issues of the arms trade. First this trade is, by its very nature, dependent on a high level of military hostilities, without which the demand for armaments would surely fall. Suppliers of arms to countries involved in conflicts, such as Israel and some Arab states, can hardly claim to be working towards a peaceful settlement in those regions. There is no single government involved in the Middle East arms race which is not publicly committed to a peaceful solution, yet it is hard to deny that the activities of the arms salesmen, who provide the means by which hostilities can be continued, negate the often-proclaimed objectives of foreign policy. This is not to suggest that the supply of arms is *of itself* the cause of unrest, but there can be little doubt that the levels of military supply can have an effect on the intensity, duration and even initiation of hostilities. The suppliers cannot blandly stand aside and disclaim all responsibility for the ultimate use of their weapons. This is particularly the case where arms sales are provided as an alternative to the direct military involvement of the supplier nation. Countries engaged in this kind of behaviour are simply hypocritical in their earnest declarations of non-involvement in wars fuelled by their actions.

Yet it is not only in areas of international tension that weapons are in demand. They are also needed by the leaders of repressive régimes as a substitute for democratic consent to their rule. It is therefore no coincidence that Iran, Saudi Arabia and Oman should be among the biggest purchasers of British arms. Indeed, it is clear that the very existence of certain repressive régimes is largely dependent upon the force of arms. A Labour Government – or any government – should not find itself in a position where it provides the means of repression. Moreover, the inherent instability of such régimes will often lead to their demise, and it is an open question as to how their new rulers will view trading relations with those who supplied weapons to their former oppressors. Even if the arms exported to countries with repressive régimes are not actually used, they serve as a deterrent to the opposition and contribute to the prestige and status of the rulers.

Most governments claim that they allow arms sales only to 'friendly' nations, and that this in itself provides a contribution to the objectives of their foreign policy. In practice, this concept is highly questionable, since there is little guarantee that the friends of today will not become the enemies of tomorrow. There are innumerable examples of arms sales to countries which have, after a change of régime, turned their weapons against the supplier nation. Even during the First World War, British guns supplied to Turkey were responsible for the deaths of British soldiers in the Dardanelles; and, today, the British provision of submarines to fascist Chile[4] is a constant reminder of the transitory nature of certain alliances. This experience is not unique to Britain. The Americans in South-East Asia have become virtually the main military supporter for some of the new Communist régimes, and the USSR has found its weapons backing the increasingly pro-Western régimes of the Egyptians, Sudanese and Syrians.

It is also necessary to consider the effect of arms sales to Third World countries in more general terms. Arms sales create a state of military dependence. They draw Third World countries into the global confrontation, and play an important role in imposing or preserving the international division of labour in peripheral economies. It was in general as a consequence of armed force that the objectives of production were shifted from local self-sufficiency to the world market in colonial countries. And today, the political and repressive role of armed forces is often important in carrying out a 'development' strategy which involves heavy emphasis on industrial growth and foreign investment at the expense of meeting basic needs.

Typical examples of the correlation between high military spending, foreign dependence, industrial growth and extreme inequality (which might be measured crudely by reference to the rate of infant mortality) are Brazil, South Korea, the Philippines and the Middle Eastern countries. This political aspect of arms sales is just as important in its impact on 'development' as the direct absorption of resources, particularly scarce foreign exchange, which might otherwise have contributed to the elimination of poverty. We would not, however, suggest that the Third World should be subject to special arms sales control before similar action had been taken in relation to the industrialized nations. The whole question is very complex, and there is a need for a wider study of the effect of arms sales on Third World economies.

Another feature of the arms trade which has recently come into sharp focus is the high level of attendant corruption. The Lockheed and Northrop scandals, to name but two, have had tremendous political repercussions in the USA, Japan, Holland and Germany. The relationship between corruption and the arms trade is hardly coincidental, for few comparable commercial transactions are surrounded by such secrecy, involve

102

such vast sums or are so dependent on the decisions of a single purchaser. This is not to say that the problem of corruption is necessarily endemic, but there needs to be some serious thinking about the way in which arms procurement decisions are taken in some countries.

Finally, it would be quite inadequate to pursue a discussion about the arms trade without considering the moral aspect. Ultimately, the arms trade is nothing more or less than the export of instruments of death, and for this reason it is really not good enough for the arms traders to argue their case in purely economic terms. The economic and moral arguments are inseparable. A court of law does not accept the plea of a drug pusher who says 'If I did not sell them, then others would', and neither should we.

A temporary loss of some military exports is a small price to pay if it helps to avoid the much greater losses that could be caused by fuelling regional disputes which could develop into a Third World War.

The Economic Argument
It is estimated that 70,000 to 80,000 jobs[5] in the United Kingdom are directly involved in the export of defence equipment, and that many other jobs are indirectly affected. The total value of arms exports in 1975/6 was £530 million,[6] which is substantial indeed when set against the budget for domestic procurement in that year, estimated at £1,853 million.

Chapter 3 of this study showed how there are many misconceptions about the economic benefits of arms exports. In the first place, current levels of military expenditure produce an overall deficit on the foreign exchange side of our military account. Secondly, the same industries which produce both civil and military goods have proved themselves to be more efficient at exporting in the civil sector, despite the consumption of valuable resources by the military. Thirdly, the deployment of high levels of investment and R & D resources by the military sector is partly responsible for hindering the development of British industry in general. It can also be seen that the firms which export most are least likely to be affected by defence cuts. The main items of military equipment included in our procurement programme are the least successful in the world market. The basis of our arms trade consists of such items as fast patrol boats, light aircraft, including helicopters, trainers and armoured cars and so forth. The problem is therefore not so

103

much one of concern about the possible loss of economic opportunities from reducing the arms trade but of concern with the present loss of export opportunities in the civil sphere.

Against this point of view, it is argued that Britain has a clear comparative advantage in the production of arms for the world market and that we would be foolish to relinquish this position. There are said to be three main benefits of the arms trade. First, that arms exports lower the unit costs of production for our own needs. Secondly, that arms exports help to maintain a high level of industrial capacity and R & D capability which would be either idle or non-existent without the arms trade. And thirdly, most sales of military goods tend to aid the sales of civil products like commercial vehicles and earth-moving equipment, particularly where the military play a large role in the governments of recipient countries.

While it is certainly true that arms exports help to maintain a high level of industrial capacity, this in itself poses some serious problems. As Chapter 3 demonstrated, it is the existence of a capacity to produce armaments that distorts a rational approach to procurement decisions. The real reason for the tremendous effort directed towards military exports is the acute and continual problem of surplus capacity in the British armaments industry. It is significant that the formation of the Defence Sales Organization (the Export Promotion Department of the Ministry of Defence) in January 1966 coincided with the last serious attempt to restrain defence expenditure. If this is the real reason for promoting arms exports, does the contention that such sales subsidize the defence budget by reducing unit costs stand up to analysis? The answer must be a qualified 'no', since no evidence has ever been produced to back this claim.

The Ministry of Defence not only refuses to place a value on its own procurement contracts, but declines to answer questions on either the value or content of individual sales to foreign governments. So long as they withhold such information, the argument that longer runs significantly reduce unit costs must remain an assumption rather than a judgement based on evidence. Such evidence as does exist in the public domain tends to confirm this impression. A study by the Stockholm International Peace Research Institute (SIPRI), for example, has shown that in general the cost of producing a typical military aircraft is only marginally reduced in the early stages of a production run, and that any benefits at a later stage (after, say, 500 units have been produced) are probably exaggerated. This is particularly so when it is remembered that most export models require some form of modification which increases unit costs.[8] Another study by the US Congressional Budget Office supports the conclusion that R & D recoveries and lower production costs are mainly associated with the purchase of new aircraft and missiles which account for a relatively small proportion of arms sales both in the US and Britain.[9] Furthermore, such savings have to be offset against the additional costs which lead from the strain on resources from meeting foreign demands at an early stage of production. In Britain, the pressure of export demand was one reason Vickers had to sub-contract a Type 42 destroyer, HMS *Cardiff*, to Swan Hunter for completion at considerable additional cost to the Ministry of Defence.[10]

Setting aside the arguments relating to the situation as it exists at present, there is some doubt about the future levels of demand for British arms abroad. On the one hand, there is a tendency for purchasers of British arms in Iran and Egypt, for example, to buy not the products themselves but manufacturing plant, design and technical know-how, thus reducing the actual demand for British-made hardware. On the other hand, there is evidence that internal pressure by US arms manufacturers on their government will lead to an insistence by the United States on a larger American share of the NATO weapons market. Should arms sales fall off as a result of these factors, there will be a strong incentive to increase domestic spending to keep these industries in activity. A further irony of the situation is that some recipients of arms-producing capability then use their acquired know-how to compete with, or embarrass politically, the original exporting nation in third markets – as has happened, for example, in the attempted export of Israeli-made military aircraft (the Kfir) to Ecuador.

This view is challenged by those who see a running down of arms purchase as being most unlikely, particularly by smaller nations unable to maintain their own industries; and as far as NATO is concerned they see moves towards a collective Euro-group procurement policy as a guarantee for maintaining the British share of the market. Yet, far from being beneficial to our domestic requirements, there is evidence that the export market's demands are in fact of no help whatsoever, and may indeed adversely influence procurement decisions. Is the £85 million being spent on the Maritime Harrier, for example, justified solely on grounds of domestic requirements? 'For a long time no government spokesman claimed it to be anything more than a "useful additional capability" – it has now been promoted to the status of "essential" '; yet this aircraft is considered to have tremendous export potential. The fact is that we shall ourselves have to use anything that we wish to sell to others, and so foreign confidence in the Maritime Harrier, for example, can be gained only if it is ordered by our own Ministry of Defence.

This argument can be taken a stage further when we consider that it is because of a high level of export orders that it is possible in the first place to consider domestic purchases of equipment which would not otherwise be suitable, especially in the light of the serious decisions at present facing us over priorities in public spending. Thus, while it may be argued that we may save money by spreading costs, the saving is illusory since it ignores the high levels of initial investment necessary to create the kind of economies of scale that are worth while. The proposition can even be turned on its head, and we shall see that purchasers of equipment already in production may well be receiving subsidized goods, the historic costs of R & D and production having already been met by the supplier nation.

The Labour Party acknowledges the possibility of some diminution in the overall level of exports in the transitional period. Set against this, however, is the potential for import substitution in other spheres which should lessen the impact on our overall balance of payments. There is also a good prospect of freeing existing industrial capacity devoted to military production for expansion into new export markets. Seen in this light, releasing British industry from the defence burden can only be a benefit; the arms trade may provide some incidental bonus to our balance of payments, but it is a most inefficient means of achieving such an objective.

How Can the Arms Trade be Controlled?

Current British Government policy for achieving arms control emphasizes the need for a multilateral agreement involving arms importers as well as exporters, possibly on a regional basis.[11] This seems to be a sensible approach as far as it goes, but we believe that the most effective way of introducing criteria for the limitation of arms sales would be to examine the following suggested ways of controlling the arms trade on a unilateral basis.

There should be two major criteria for an embargo on arms sales to overseas buyers. First, we could follow the German and Japanese practice of not supplying arms to states either engaged

106

in international disputes or likely to become involved in them. Secondly, and more problematic (in terms of definition), we should consider limiting arms sales to all countries which use torture and repression against their subjects. In other words, governments with a continuous record of human-rights violation should not be given the means to perpetuate their activities.

Another step which could be taken as part of the process towards control of the global arms trade would be to create a Register of Arms Sales, possibly as part of an international register, under UN auspices. Such a register would include full details of the sales as well as the names of agents and the level of their fees. A register will not in itself guarantee a reduction in the scale of the arms trade, but it should have beneficial effects both by generally breaking down the unnecessary secrecy surrounding these transactions, and by making a useful contribution to public debate on this question.

At present information on arms sales in the United Kingdom is very difficult to come by. Were it not for the activities of the Stockholm International Peace Research Institute (SIPRI) in Sweden and the Campaign Against Arms Trade in Britain, we should probably not even have access to the limited information that is available. The Director of the United States Arms Control and Disarmament Agency has stated the case for this kind of disclosure very clearly: 'My Agency,' he says, 'has made a special effort to inform the public about the flow of armaments and trends in military expenditure throughout the world . . . We feel the world public has a right to know for its vital interest is at stake.'[12]

Britain has already taken some unilateral steps towards arms control with the introduction of a licensing system. This has meant that an embargo has existed on the sale of arms to South Africa since 1974, and we are no longer accepting new orders from Chile. Even stricter controls have been in operation for much longer prohibiting sales to Warsaw Pact countries and most of their allies. Therefore proposals for extending this kind of action would not mark any major change of policy. Nevertheless, it would mean a tightening of existing regulations, since there is now, particularly in the case of South Africa, considerable evidence of British companies (notably Marconi, ICI and Raçal) circumventing the arms control legislation.[13]

None of this is to suggest that the supply of arms is in all cases wrong, or that we should withdraw entirely from the arms trade. On the contrary, we should reserve the right to provide supplies (even as aid) to countries with whom we maintain friendly relations (even accepting the fact that governments change and so do relations), especially when they are threatened by hostile powers. The central point of our proposals is to emphasize that no arms sales policy can be disinterested in its political implications, and that it is therefore essential to establish workable criteria for such sales.

There will, of course, be problems of defining what is and what is not military equipment, but it would surely not be beyond the capability of the Ministry of Defence to ensure the regulation of all sales requiring a licence under the 1970 Customs and Excise Exports of Goods (Control) Order. It would also be necessary to include those sales not requiring a licence, but whose use is likely to be military: radar, sonar detection equipment, microwave components, ionospheric and meteroric scatter radio relay communication equipment, to give a few examples.

Conclusion

The programme for a reduction in arms sales will have to be combined with a programme for industrial conversion. Implicit in the strategy for the latter is the need to cut down on arms exports. The fundamental objective of such planning should therefore be both to release economic resources and to contribute towards a lessening of tension in what is, at present, a militarily overstocked world.

Notes and References

1. For a breakdown of British arms exports, see Campaign Against Arms Trade, Factsheets available from CAAT, 5 Caledonian Road, London N1 9DX.
2. Dr Iklé, speech at the Conference of the Committee on Disarmament, 29 July 1976.
3. Interview with Henry Brandon, *Sunday Times*, 30 January 1977.
4. The original order was placed with the 'friendly' Christian Democratic government of President Frei. Between the time of ordering and final delivery, there have been two significant changes of government.
5. *Hansard*, 19 October 1976, cols. 421–2.
6. *Hansard*, 24 January 1977, col. 502.
7. *Statement on the Defence Estimates, 1976*, Cmnd 6432, p. 48. (This figure is given at 1976/7 Estimates Prices.)
8. See *The Arms Trade and the Third World*, SIPRI, Stockholm, 1971, p. 400. Further discussion of this question is to be found in ibid., Ch. 14.
9. 'Foreign Military and US Weapons Costs', Staff Working Paper, 5 May, 1976, Congressional Budget Office, Washington, DC.
10. See Appendix IX in the full report for details.

108

11. See Speech by the Rt Hon. Lord Goronwy Roberts in the First Committee of the United Nations XXXIst General Assembly, 2 November 1976.
12. Dr Iklé, as n. 2 above.
13. See *Black South Africa Explodes*, Counter-Information Services, London, 1976, p. 49.

Two Case-studies

One: TORNADO, THE MULTI-ROLE COMBAT AIRCRAFT (MRCA)

Part 1: Background to the Project

MRCA, the aircraft known as Tornado, is a collaborative project involving Britain, Italy and the Federal Republic of Germany (FRG). When MRCA is finally produced it will make up about half the RAF's combat capability in the 1980s; it is intended to replace Canberra, Buccaneer, Vulcan and, eventually, Phantom. It is the major military aerospace project for Britain at the present time.

Organization
In July, 1968 Belgium, Britain, Canada, the FRG, Italy and the Netherlands initialled a Memorandum of Understanding declaring their interest in the development of a multi-role variable geometry aircraft. Within a year, Belgium, Canada and the Netherlands had withdrawn from the project, apparently because of the expense and complications of the project, both technically and organizationally.

In March 1969, Panavia was formed. It is a consortium of BAC, MBB and Fiat; BAC and MBB each now have a 42·5 per cent share in Panavia, Fiat has 15 per cent. Panavia is subordinate to the NATO MRCA Management Organization (NAMMO), which oversees the whole project. NAMMO's instructions are carried out by the NATO MRCA Management Agency (NAMMA), which functions as NAMMO's executive body and also pays the sub-contractors. Panavia and NAMMA each have a staff of about 140.

NAMMO and NAMMA function on behalf of the three governments; Panavia is a German company, subservient to German company law, with an international board of six directors appointed from member companies.[1]

The engine – the RB199 – is being produced by Turbo-Union, a consortium of Rolls-Royce (40 per cent share), MTU (40 per cent), and Aeritalia (20 per cent).

Panavia is responsible for the airframe, and for coordinating the activities of Turbo-Union and Avionica (the company responsible for the avionics).

Contracts for work have been carefully divided into systems and sub-systems, and in some cases sub-sub-systems, and allotted on a basis reflecting the interest of each government in the project. In the airframe, BAC is responsible for the nose and rear fuselage, MBB for the centre fuselage including the wing joints (despite its lack of previous experience in this the most sensitive part of a swing-wing aircraft), and Fiat for the wings. Responsibility for the engine has been divided up in a similar fashion. Each contractor sub-contracts out; many of the sub-contractors are involved in work-sharing arrangements.

Each country will have its own production line and assemble aircraft from the components provided by the various sub-contractors.

British, German and Italian firms are participating in the development of each and every system in the aircraft.[2]

The British will be developing an Interceptor variant alone (see below).

Timetables
Project definition was completed in 1970 and development begun. The intention was that the first prototype should fly in September 1973; the nine pre-production models would all have flown by September 1975, and the aircraft was expected to enter service around the end of 1977.[3]

By May 1972 the delay on sending out contracts (because of the large number of permutations possible) had delayed the programme six months and the service entry date was accordingly deferred into early 1978.[4] In September 1972, the maiden flight was put back three months to December 1973. There were several more delays before the maiden flight finally took place on 15 August 1974, nearly a year behind schedule.

In October 1974, after a review of the project, the British MoD announced approval for the project through to December 1975, when production orders would be placed. It is unlikely that the pre-production models will fly for some time.

When the White Paper on the Defence Estimates was published in March 1975, the Interceptor variant was in the project definition stage.[5]

Numbers
In 1970, Mr B. O. Heath, the MRCA project manager at BAC, believed that total orders would lead to a likely production figure of 'over 1,000 aeroplanes, nearly 1,200'.[6]

In 1972, after various other estimates had been eliminated, the generally agreed figure was a total of around 900 – a maximum of 420 for FRG, 350 to 400 for Britain, and around 100 for Italy.[7] In August 1972, the FRG reduced its order to 320 because of rising costs;[8] the order now stands at 320 for the FRG, 385 for Britain and 100 for Italy.

The RAF's 385 is made up of about 165 of the Interceptor variant, and 220 of the so-called 'common MRCA'.[9]

Roles and characteristics
MRCA will be required to fulfil five roles for three air forces:
(a) Strike and interdiction (including naval strike) – for RAF and Luftwaffe.
(b) Close air support – for all three.
(c) Reconnaissance – for all three.
(d) Air defence interception – for RAF.
(e) Air superiority – for Luftwaffe and IAF.[10]

To perform all these roles, the aircraft requires seventeen basic characteristics (see appendix to this paper, p. 117), plus a flexible armaments-carrying ability.

The Interceptor is regarded as a separate aircraft from the 'common MRCA' which will perform the other roles; however, it will have the same basic airframe and the same engine. Aerodynamic modifications, and the removal of certain avionic systems to reduce weight, are the major changes envisaged for the Interceptor.[11]

The requirements of the different versions are in some cases conflicting. For example, the Interceptor needs an engine capable of high thrust, while the others need long range/duration, i.e. low fuel consumption. The short take-off and landing (STOL) necessary for the 'common MRCA' calls for an unswept wing, while low-level supersonic speed needs a swept wing; STOL needs a low wing loading while low-level speed needs high wing

115

loading, but maximum manoeuvrability calls for a moderate wing loading.[12]

Different versions of MRCA will have abilities they do not need – 'wasted characteristics'. For example, the RAF will have a strike aircraft capable of high manoeuvrability and cab-rank loitering; it will have a close support bomber capable of supersonic speeds at low level, and a reconnaissance aircraft with a fast rate of climb.

The swing-wing airframe and the turbofan RB199 engine appear to be the way to reconcile the conflicting requirements, but it does seem somewhat profligate to waste characteristics in this way, especially since each one costs money and real resources. From the appendix (p. 117) it will be noted that there is only one characteristic shared by all versions of MRCA; even within the 'common' version, sharing is not particularly high.

It is the technical sophistication and innovation required to reconcile the conflicts and provide all the characteristics which have resulted in the high costs of the MRCA. In addition, real increases in the unit cost probably stem from this factor. Anything innovative on such a large scale is a risky project, and the increased costs resulting from hitches is multiplied by the size of the bureaucracy controlling the project, the committee method of taking development decisions (itself likely to cause delay), and the inflexible development strategy employed.[13]

Conclusions
(1) The three governments set out on a project to succeed where others had failed, and with a necessity for sophistication and innovation. This, together with the collaborative method, has pushed costs up.
(2) Given the economic circumstances and the limited progress made thus far on the Interceptor variant, there seems every possibility that it will be cancelled – which will increase unit costs on the other versions.
(3) Cancellation of production *in toto* seems less likely but possible.
(4) The problems encountered in this project should inspire extreme caution about other collaborative projects.

DAN SMITH

Appendix to paper: Roles and characteristics
Characteristics required, together with the roles to which they attach, are as follows:

116

All-weather operation: All roles
Long range/duration: All except Interceptor
Transonic low-level speed: Strike/interdiction
Large weapon load ability: Strike/interdiction
High navigation accuracy: Strike: Close support; Reconnaissance
Accurate weapon delivery: Strike; Close support
Good subsonic handling: Close support
Recce equipment carriage: Reconnaissance
Rapid data evaluation: Reconnaissance
Good manoeuvrability at low and medium level: Air superiority
Rapid acceleration: Interceptor
High rate of climb: Interceptor
Supersonic cruise: Interceptor
Maximum manoeuvrability: Interceptor
Target acquisition and identification: Interceptor
STOL: Strike; Close Support; reconnaissance
Low speed for 'cab-rank' loitering: Air superiority

In some cases, the characteristic will be acquired for the aircraft
by the addition or removal of certain avionic systems. In other
cases, where the characteristics apply to the engine or the basic
airframe (as in cases of speed, manoeuvrability and load), various
versions will have 'wasted characteristics'; the engine will be
capable of all the various abilities, and the airframe able to stand
up to all the different types of stresses to which it will be sub-
jected in its various roles.

Notes and References
 1. W. B. Walker, 'The *MRCA*: a Case Study in European Collabora-
    tion', *Research Policy*, 2 (1974).
 2. As n. 1.
 3. As n. 1; and *Flight International*, 4 May 1972.
 4. As n. 3.
 5. *1975 Defence Estimates*, White Paper, ch. VII, para. 12.
 6. Quoted in Walker, art. cit.
 7. *Interavia*, April 1972.
 8. *Aviation Week and Space Technology*, 11 September 1972.
 9. *Flight International*, 28 March 1974.
10. See *Interavia*, April 1973; *Flight International*, 28 March 1974; and
    White Paper, March 1975, ch. VII, para. 11.
11. *Flight International*, 28 March 1974.
12. *Interavia*, April 1973.
13. See Walker, art. cit., for a fuller discussion.

(The author is indebted to the Institute of Strategic Studies for use of
their facilities in the preparation of the paper.)

Part 2: Conversion and
Diversification in the Aerospace
Industry in the Event of
Tornado's Cancellation

The discussion in this paper outlines recent developments in the Tornado saga, and, although cancellation is viewed as extremely unlikely, considers the conversion potential embodied in the resources devoted to that project. During the discussion, two terms are used which should be understood separately. *Conversion* refers to the process by which part of our military aerospace capacity would move into a different field of manufacture – a once and for all change; *diversification*, relating to unconverted capacity, implies that other work could be alternated with aerospace development and production. The conditions under which diversification might be possible are discussed in the paper.

Tornado
Approval for production of the 'common' version (IDS) MRCA Tornado was announced on 5 March 1976; 220 will be produced, and the intention to order 165 copies of the British-only Air Defence Variant (ADV) was confirmed, and full development approved.

Tornado costs remain a matter for controversy. The government quotes £6·34 million as the IDS unit cost, and £7·72 million for the ADV (1977/8 estimate prices), but it is not clear that the cost of R & D is included in either figure; it has also been suggested that the ADV's air-to-air missiles, without which it is hardly a weapon system, are excluded from the figures.

Briefly, the 'life-time' cost per copy for the IDS is calculated at £16·81 million, and for the ADV at £20·22 million; this gives a 'life-time' cost for the whole project and the full order of 385 aircraft in the region of £7,000 million. This estimate is higher than estimates generally made by even the severest critics of Tornado – estimates above about £4,000 million have not normally been seen. Of course, these estimates are in 1975 prices, and actual cash outlay will be vastly higher over the period of fifteen years.

On the basis of these estimates, the budget outlay on Tornado for the years 1978/9 to 1980/81 will be somewhere over £250 million for each year. Should ADV production begin in 1980/81, which seems a little early given present progress, then the outlay for the second of those years might be around £300 million, and for the third closer to £350 million. These figures are more or less compatible with those suggested by David Greenwood.[1]

Estimating cancellation costs is extremely difficult because of the paucity of data. Nor is it possible to use costs for cancelling previous projects (e.g. TSR-2) as a guide, because work on Tornado is so much further advanced. Tooling-up has begun at the BAC plant in Preston where the aircraft will be assembled, with full production likely to get under way in 1978. This advanced stage alone makes it virtually impossible that Tornado will be cancelled – or the IDS version, at any rate; it might still be possible to stop the ADV, not only because it is less advanced but because it is a British-only project. As a case-study, the survey of conversion prospects arising from cancellation of Tornado remains useful, but barring something unforeseeable, the RAF will be equipped with the IDS version at least in the 1980s. Of the eventual outlay on the ADV, only the development investment is irretrievably committed; ADV cancellation would probably mean 'losing' a little over the total development cost (i.e. somewhere above £225 million), but with important resources saved, although the longer one waits the more expensive cancellation will become.

Recently there has been growing criticism of Tornado in the press and elsewhere, dealing not with the project's basic desirability or suitability, but with its alleged deficiencies in two categories – weaponry and performance.

The former was the subject of a short debate in the House of Commons, raised by Ronald Brown, MP, concerning contract procedure for the main weapons computer, euphemistically known as the 'stores management system'.[2] He complained that

Marconi-Elliott Avionics Systems Ltd (MEASL), while prime contractor for the system, was unable to fulfil the specifications, but, when the contract was re-offered for tender, the British and Italian governments reselected MEASL, although the FRG opted for an American company, Base Ten.

Whatever the propriety of MEASL getting a second chance, the failure of its first effort has meant a delay of four years; in addition, Base Ten and MEASL are reported to be working on two completely different and incompatible systems. If production and delivery schedules are maintained, both contractors have extremely tight schedules for their work. Replying to the debate, the Minister of State placed the blame for the failure not on MEASL, but on the governments' insufficiently detailed and over-ambitious specifications.[3] Indeed, given Tornado's small size and multiplicity of roles (resulting in a wide range of tasks for the computer), MEASL's job was like fitting a quart into a pint pot. One might, however, argue that MEASL should have assessed the task more carefully before taking it on.

It is alleged that the aircraft's RB-199 engine is not producing the thrust it should, although the reported scope of the failure depends upon the source. *Air et Cosmos*, a French journal, suggests Tornado will fly no faster than Mach 1.3, while Interavia has estimated a maximum speed of Mach 1.7.[4] Other sources have suggested that the engine's present thrust can produce an airspeed of Mach 1.4, but that continued work should get it up to Mach 1.8. All these speeds are below BAC's claim of Mach 2, and below the Mach 2.2 originally advertised for the ADV.

The relatively low speed is not a worry in relation to Tornado's close support or battlefield interdiction roles, where the emphasis is on pinpoint accuracy rather than speed. It is, however, a matter of concern for the long-range strike, deep interdiction, reconnaissance and interceptor roles. By way of comparison, the Mig-25 Foxbat, which recently sneaked into Japan, and which performs as both interceptor and reconnaissance aircraft, is reportedly capable of speeds of Mach 2.8.[5]

Should the problems with the engine be ironed out, there is yet another snag, brought to light by Stephen Thornley, an aviation scientist sacked for his criticisms of Tornado. Apparently, the variable air-intake on the fuselage has been mal-designed, so that whatever thrust the engine produces, the aircraft will be incapable of speeds above Mach 2, and probably not even that high.

With Tornado far from completed, it seems that the sequel is ready to run. Air Staff Target (AST) 403, generally discussed as a replacement for Harrier and Jaguar, may eventually result in another collaborative project on the scale of Tornado.

To the Expenditure Committee, MoD officials commented that plans for a new fighter aircraft are 'under consideration'; without being drawn, they implied that the aircraft would be neither a Tornado derivative, nor the American F-15 Eagle, but probably a completely new aircraft.[6] It has been suggested that AST-403 is conceived of primarily as a bomber which could also fulfil various fighter roles.[7] If this is so, and if the MoD officials' remarks concerned AST-403, and if it is not to be bought off the shelf from the USA, then, even at this early stage, and with such incomplete evidence, there are grounds for concern. It is the view of General Dynamics, prime contractors for the F-16, that 'it is possible to adapt an air-to-air fighter for ground attack, but not vice versa'; it could be that AST-403 is starting back to front.[8]

There must also be severe doubts about the efficiency both of the multi-role concept, when taken to the lengths it has been in Tornado, and of the collaborative framework for development and production. Leaving aside the more profound political implications of collaborative projects, it does appear that costs are increased by collaboration. It causes a proliferation of roles, requiring differing and sometimes conflicting performance characteristics, which all have to be fitted in at great cost and with the consequences we have considered in MEASL's inability to fulfil the specifications; this causes delay, and extra cost. It also makes the project extremely hard to keep under effective control – by many, this last criticism is seen as the most powerful argument *in favour* of collaboration, since cancellation becomes harder. The multi-role concept, adopted because of continuing and staggering cost increases for advanced weaponry, aims at having one aircraft perform a variety of tasks, which results in a product unnecessarily sophisticated for each task, often performing less effectively than a specialized aircraft would, and still enormously expensive. Tornado has been sarcastically but relevantly described as 'the egg-laying, wool-producing, milk-giving sow' – it may be nice to have sows laying eggs, but hens do the same thing more easily and cheaply.[9] And it is no longer certain that all the roles that aircraft now fulfil are relevant, desirable or necessary or possible in the 1980s and beyond; there are strong reasons for thinking that in a rapidly changing strategic environment aircraft can and should have a more limited range of tasks in the future.[10]

Before the decision is taken to embark upon a new multi-role collaborative project which will again develop almost unstoppable momentum, there should be a much closer and more critical examination of the experience and issues involved in Tornado. Its one potential benefit is as a warning against such gross waste of resources in the future. Government assertions that Tornado is a wonderful aircraft, and that collaboration works beautifully, just will not do.

Tornado Contractors

This long list of firms involved in Tornado work causes its own problems for a consideration of alternative work. It becomes next to impossible to quantify the workforce involved in any detail. The Government either does not have the data or is unwilling to provide them. An answer to one Parliamentary Question could provide only a limited list of contractors, while another could not provide the division of skills in the workforce, the regions in which they are employed, or the numbers presently employed, apart from 5,500 at BAC and 4,000 at Rolls-Royce.[11]

It is thus impossible to define with any precision the details of the conversion and diversification task consequent upon cancellation of Tornado. Accordingly, our discussion deals in terms of possibilities and suggestions, rather than a blueprint. Since the Corporate Plan of the Lucas Aerospace Shop Stewards Combine Committee provides such an exceptional range of alternatives for the aerospace equipment industry, the discussion is limited to airframe and aeroengine – to BAC and Rolls-Royce.

Conversion and Diversification and the Aerospace Industry

British aerospace, along with the rest of West European aerospace, is in a profound crisis. Since 1968, BAC's civil aviation division has announced mass redundancies on no less than seven occasions. In civil aviation in particular, European firms suffer blow after blow at the hands of their American rivals who have tremendous advantages through economy of scale and the size of their domestic market (even though US aerospace is far from trouble-free). The EEC Action Plan for European Aerospace asserted that without decisive collective action by European aerospace firms and governments, European aerospace would wither away to nothing.[12] But although the distinctly federalist tinge of the proposals might have the profoundest implications for government relations, its effects on civil aerospace at least might be little more than cosmetic, which may explain the delay in implementing the plan's proposals, and the apparent low interest in projects such as the European Airbus.[13]

Unfortunately for the industry, no long-term solution to its problems can be found in military aerospace manufacture, which would, anyway, leave civil aerospace workers redundant. The problems of the industry are not so much to do with bad management or selling techniques, as with the difficulties created by expanding capacity and escalating costs, in a strategic environment in which their military wares' roles are increasingly threatened and may not be viable at costs which are anything like acceptable.

Even if Tornado survives, conversion of military aerospace capacity remains important – for the workers in the industry, for allocation of resources, and for the development of more coherent defence policy better tailored to our economic capacity.

However, a programme of conversion should not merely consider alternative development production, but also the extent to which parts of the industry should be maintained in their present form, or even perhaps expanded, for two main reasons.

There will certainly be a continuing requirement for military aircraft to perform certain missions, and the appropriate development and production capacity would therefore need to be maintained (barring a decision to purchase all military aircraft from abroad). Additionally, it should be noted that Rolls-Royce maintains a dominating position in the EEC aeroengine industry – it is larger than all its EEC rivals put together. While this is not an argument for excluding Rolls-Royce from conversion planning, it would clearly be foolish to discard an industry in which Britain has such a strong advantage.

What is needed is therefore not only conversion of capacity superfluous to our requirements, but also a measure of diversification to provide the retained industry with greater stability and security, with the added advantage of potentially reducing the cost of maintaining development and production capacity for military aerospace, in periods when there is no major procurement under way. This possibility is discussed in more detail below.

Despite spirited opposition from the House of Lords during the debate on airframe nationalization, the new nationalized airframe corporation does have the statutory possibility of diversifying manufacture, if the order by the Secretary of State is approved by both Houses of Parliaments.[14] Given the Lords' opposition to this during their attempts to mutilate the Bill, one may fear the corporation would not be permitted to diversify; however, the motive behind the Lords' amendment to this part

123

of the Bill was apparently the fear of the Society of British Aerospace Companies that the nationalized industry would compete with or absorb ancillary manufacturers, and the most desirable diversification would not be into that area, but into completely new product fields.[15] The Act also contains clauses obliging the corporation 'to promote industrial democracy in a strong and organic form', which could be most important in helping to ensure wide involvement in the planning process which the Study Group has recognized as so important.[16]

Conversion and Diversification at BAC and Rolls-Royce
Cancellation of Tornado now would release in excess of 5,500 workers at BAC and 4,000 at Rolls-Royce, plus plant space and machinery, for alternative work.[17] It would also affect the job prospects of a further 4,500 at BAC, and 2,000 at Rolls-Royce, who can expect to be employed on Tornado when work is at its peak.[18] If associated development capacity were also converted or diversified, the number affected would be much greater.

We can be fairly sure that the alternative products discussed below are far from constituting a complete list of conversion and diversification options for these workers. Although the bulk of the suggestions come from the workforce, at neither BAC nor Rolls-Royce has there been the kind of systematic search for alternatives which was undertaken at Lucas Aerospace. While the BAC Combine Committee has considered the question of diversification, largely as a fall-back should redundancies loom, it has not done so in detail; in Rolls-Royce, suggestions are circulating for discussion, but the process has gone no further. We can be reasonably sure that a much larger range of alternatives would be produced were the task to be taken on systematically.

However, there are in BAC suggestions that a strategy be adopted, similar to that which underlies the Lucas Aerospace Corporate Plan, to develop Job Protection Agreements rather than fighting each redundancy as it emerges. This would be based on a five- to ten-year plan, with full information available about investment intentions and possibilities, aimed at providing alternative production during dips in military aerospace production (as between Jaguar and Tornado). Thus, production would be alternated between one type of manufacture and another. This plan, possible in a nationalized industry, but only with effective industrial democracy and advance planning, would aim at providing security where now there is only the fear of

124

redundancy whenever production of an aircraft is wound down.

However, it would not be possible to alternate production in this way if it were suggested that the entire plant be switched away from military aerospace, then back to it, then away, and so on. As these ideas are developing, therefore, they envisage the maintenance of a skilled 'pool' of labour constantly involved with whatever types of production were undertaken. Production lines would need to 'tick over' whenever they were not operating at full pressure; this already happens at BAC (on Canberra and Jaguar, for example) so it is nothing new. The weight of the workforce could then be directed wherever necessary, but the basic capability would not be lost. To some extent, this does already happen at BAC: teams have, for example, worked on helicopters or submarines for periods instead of on fixed-wing aircraft.

While this kind of alternating production would provide greater security and stability, and while the concept has potential not only for BAC but also for Rolls-Royce, there are two particularly important factors which limit the scope of the proposal.

Non-military aerospace production would have to be in fields employing closely related skills, or the 'learning' period at the start of new aircraft production would be lengthened and costs accordingly increased; at the extreme, the skills might have to be totally relearned unless the other types of work were in compatible fields. While it is not particularly difficult to identify work with the appropriate compatible skills, this is a factor limiting the range of options.

More importantly, alternating production in this way would appear to rule out the non-military part of the enterprise being in a field which involves competition on the open market. In a competitive and rapidly changing market, it is, first, difficult to get a foot in the door; once there, a full effort is necessary to maintain the position. Therefore, the non-military part of the alternating production should be making things for which the Government is the market, and the fields which offer themselves for consideration are such as energy, health, transport or education.

Should it be decided, as it is reasonable to suppose it will, that a continued military aerospace industrial capacity is required, the Government will either come under pressure to keep that capacity in full business by constantly procuring newer and 'better' aircraft (and this would be so whether or not the industry were nationalized), or it will, more sensibly, find cheaper ways of

125

maintaining that capacity. It could do this by going against all precedent and deciding not to go for completely new aircraft, concentrating instead on continued marginal improvements on already established types. This appears to be happening to some extent with the Chieftain tank, and with the French main battle tank, the AMX-30. But the two main weaknesses of this plan are that, if it started from Tornado, it would be beginning on a very unsound basis, and that limits of improvement might quite frequently be reached; however, it remains worth considering whether each replacement generation of aircraft *has* to be so utterly different from its predecessor. Alternatively, in times when the Government did not require new or further aircraft, it could wind production on aircraft down and provide other kinds of work. Thus the costs of maintaining the capacity would be offset by also using it to produce other things we really need.

Essentially, then, we are talking about a three-part process:

(a) Establish a level of development and production capacity needed for military aircraft, compatible with our economic capacity and strategic requirement;
(b) Convert the rest of the present capacity to other kinds of work;
(c) Diversify the remaining aerospace capacity, creating a basic minimum for aerospace, a minimum for other types of production, and, so to speak, a 'floating' workforce.

At first consideration, there do not seem insurmountable barriers to development staff being 'mobile' in the same way as production workers. The need to have compatible production skills in all parts of the alternating production has already been discussed; this would mean that the underlying technology of the products need not change – the ends to which it would be put are different. Development staffs' experience in such fields as stress in materials and structures, hydraulics, components, electronics, instrumentation and production and assembly techniques, could be applied equally to the military and the other types of production. Where parts of the development tasks on the non-military projects demanded different skills, there could be a measure of occupational conversion, or, more simply, new staff could be brought in.

It will be readily admitted that all of this involves a major planning task, with government prepared to co-ordinate its procurement policy and timetables between departments. However, the alternative, with or without defence cuts, is the threat of

126

unemployment, often coming true, a continued waste of resources, and the creation of surplus capacity which will continue to confuse weapons procurement decisions. If, in the event of defence cuts, the unconverted capacity were not diversified, we should, by reducing capacity, have reduced the problems generated by capacity expansion, but it would remain a problem creating constant pressure for higher military budgets; we would be better off than we are now, but, by diversifying, we could be better off still. The ideas emerging in BAC along these lines, while not as developed as those which have emerged from Lucas Aerospace, do thus provide a reasonable basis on which to proceed.

Alternative Products

In seeking alternative products, we start from the basis of looking for work which is socially and/or economically valuable, representing a sensible use of resources, contributing either to government social programmes, or to the general strength of the economy. To fulfil the latter aim we should be thinking about products which can be import substitutes or have export potential (or both). While converted capacity may need support from government over a possibly quite lengthy period, it could and should aspire to competitiveness. As suggested above, diversified capacity will need to find safer and less volatile markets – essentially, the government through its various programmes, and possibly local authorities.

The process of conversion and diversification cannot be viewed in isolation, nor should it be seen as a purely technical issue. In following sections, the discussion raises related areas of policy – adopting some of the alternative products below would require important decisions over the National Health Service, energy or transport, for example – and the need for industrial restructuring, so that managerial and development methods and organization are appropriate to the new fields of enterprise. It should also be realized that making converted capacity competitive involves public investment in areas of profitable manufacture, along the lines already worked out for Labour's industrial strategy.[19] Support from the Government while competitiveness is established does not just mean financial aid; it could also require steps such as preferential purchasing by nationalized industry or selective import controls (on machine tools, for example). A more vigorous implementation of the planning agreement system could also be required for both conversion and diversification. These are political decisions

127

which could be part and parcel of a successful transfer of resources. The technical issues are important, but they only have real meaning against a political background.

Full use of resources involves identifying work which most benefits from those resources. In the airframe industry, to quote an early study, 'The primary resource of the industry is its ability to design, develop and manufacture new and advanced products.'[20] Our inquiries will be most fruitful if directed towards advanced and advancing technologies. Rolls-Royce has tremendous experience in the production of sophisticated engines of all kinds and uses, and this, together with its high potential for skilled precision work, provides us with useful guidelines for assessing alternative products.

The following examples of alternatives are drawn from three sources – one document from each of the workforces at BAC and Rolls-Royce, and the earlier paper on aerospace conversion for the Study Group.[21]

Machine tools: The decline of the British machine-tool industry is reflected not just by the fact that the majority of new tools are imported, but also by noting that virtually all the most advanced tools come from abroad (particularly from the FRG and Italy). Conversion at either BAC or Rolls-Royce, or both, could be an opportunity for boosting British manufacture of machine tools, particularly if it were decided to concentrate on the sophisticated types – with computer controls and servo-hydraulic operation. *Buns Before Gutter*[21] points out that Pratt & Whitney, the US aeroengine corporation, has converted some of its capacity to machine-tool manufacture. Rebuilding the machine-tool industry seems a basic condition of revitalizing British industry as a whole, and conversion provides an opportunity; by reducing imports it would also help the balance of payments, and might eventually provide exports.

Processing plants: Again, this work would suit both BAC and Rolls-Royce. The Recovery Works at Avonmouth has been able to reclaim, from sewage, water for industry, gas for heating and power generation, and soil conditioners. The 1976 drought makes the first of those a topical goal, but the others are equally important. Future developments are likely to provide processes for recovering proteins from fine chemicals; ethylene recovery from oil is already under way and could be further expanded. Recovery and re-use of parts of waste clearly helps to get the most

128

out of resources, and, if development and production capacity can be made available, it would be pointless to continue largely to rely on imports from the USA. With a fairly small numerical requirement and long lead times, this could be an option for diversification; should it be decided to export the products, conversion would be more suitable. Either way, Rolls-Royce could make the engines, with BAC responsible for components and assembly.

Energy: The primary market here is the Government, but, before conversion or diversification into this field, basic decisions are needed. Two particular types of production have emerged as suitable: (a) Barrage schemes: further development of tidal-power schemes, such as the Severn Barrage, would require engines which Rolls-Royce could manufacture. This has also been raised as a conversion option for Vickers Barrow, and the two places could dovetail their operations.[22] And (b) Nuclear material disposal: if we were committed to relying on nuclear power for energy generation, then every effort should be made to provide safe methods of waste disposal; airframe experience in stress technology, materials and structures could all go some way towards this.

In addition, some of the ambitious alternative energy schemes, such as solar-panel generators or windmower generators, would require assembly which could be done at BAC, particularly because, as has been shown by the Lucas Plan, aerospace technology and experience can help to turn these from visionary ideas into concrete realities.

Marine engines: This is an option for conversion at Rolls-Royce; gas-turbine engines are already successfully adapted for use in naval shipping, and it has been suggested that commercial shipping will also utilize them. One of the problems about this is that turbine engines may be too sophisticated, providing advantages which are really illusory for merchant shipping, as suggested by Mary Kaldor.[22] On the other hand, Rolls-Royce was some time ago approached by Cuba for gas turbines for its trawler fleet; it is suggested in *Buns Before Gutter*[23] that the approach led to nothing because of American pressure. There has also been considerable interest, not least in Japan, in using gas turbines in oil tankers. There might therefore be possibilities in either or both of those types of shipping, although the retraction of world trade (and thus the excess shipbuilding capacity which

129

exists world-wide) raises obvious problems. It is therefore an option to be approached with some care, but one worth detailed consideration of the possibilities and potential advantages, including a full survey of market potential; it would be foolish and frustrating for Rolls-Royce to fail to identify possibilities if they do exist, and thus miss an opportunity which would have tremendous export potential.

Freighter aircraft: It has previously been suggested that a short take-off and landing (STOL) freighter/passenger aircraft might open up a market in the Third World, where previously inaccessible parts could be reached more cheaply and easily than in such methods as building railways.[24] Naturally, such a project could be suitable for both BAC and Rolls-Royce, as well as aerospace equipment firms; it might also have military applications – the USA is now in the process of developing a STOL military transport.[25] Perhaps precisely because the USA industry is already into this field, it is an option which should be approached with care. It may be, however, that a civil STOL transport could be less sophisticated, and therefore cheaper, with advantage. Again, this requires detailed study.

Prefabricated parts for construction: This has long been regarded as one of the airframe industry's major options for conversion, but it is full of problems, some of which were discussed in *Aspects of Conversion of Arms Industries.*[26] It would mean entry into a field which is already under critical examination in the Labour Party, with fundamental reforms now being discussed.[27] Not only would there need to be an infusion into BAC of architectural talent, but also, particularly if prefab housing were taken up, an entirely new promotion and marketing organization would have to be created. For this reason, prefabrication of parts for industrial structures and, for example, bridges, might be a more attractive proposition. Any moves taking up this option would need to be planned alongside other possible reforms in the building industry.

Rolling stock: The idea of developing new types of light-weight railway rolling stock, replacing the century-old concepts now utilized, emerged from the Lucas Aerospace Combine Committee's Corporate Plan. It remained a possibility, utilizing airframe experience together with traditional coach design expertise, to develop cheaper and safer rolling stock (the present

130

rigid-structure and extremely heavy stock tends to exacerbate the effects of accidents); the hybrid road/rail vehicle which has been developed also raises attractive possibilities. It opens the possibility of drive-on drive-off rail transport; it could make track-laying cheaper by being able to take steeper gradients (and this could be suitable for use both in Britain and the Third World). With the Government as the sole purchaser, in the initial stages at least, there would be plenty of scope for planning production, so, although a good deal of R & D work would be necessary, this could be a possibility for diversification at BAC, depending upon the layout of the plant.

Medical manufacture: This is an option for either conversion or diversification at BAC, and would particularly involve production of the kind of sophisticated monitoring equipment used in intensive care units, but also of aids for the elderly, crippled and handicapped, making use of vastly simplified aerospace controls technology. This would demand a basic decision for greater investment in the National Health Service.

It has also been suggested that 'compact and efficient agricultural equipment' could be manufactured at BAC, although this would depend on numerous factors, not least the fact that the government may well be unwilling to compete against British companies already involved in the field.[28] The same source suggests that the expertise in all kinds of fields available at BAC could be used to establish a testing and advice centre for British industry; were such a centre established, it should involve other types of manufacture as well, or else be one of a series of centres. It is a useful idea, the demand for which should be assessed, but it is neither necessarily dependent upon a conversion programme, nor necessarily best situated in Preston.

Problems of Conversion and Diversification
The products above, while probably not a complete list, represent a reasonable range of conversion and diversification options – as Peter Ward puts it, 'a good starter for ten'.[29] When this list is added to others which have been reported to the Study Group together with those in the Corporate Plan for Lucas Aerospace, and even when the overlapping projects are eliminated, the list of possible alternative products for conversion and diversification in arms industries looks pretty impressive. The problems are not to do with finding alternatives.

The first problem is to do with selecting between the various alternatives. The selection must be made on the basis of suitability to existing facilities and skills, and on the basis of social and economic value. American experience in base conversion has shown the value at a community level of a proper strategy, identifying assets, requirements and constraints;[30] the same principle holds for a national conversion effort. Obviously, a good deal of preliminary work is necessary as a basis from which to plan the details.

The second problem is one of co-ordination, avoiding duplication and phasing the changeover from one kind of production to another.

Converted capacity will have to be supported during a transition period. While capacity can be converted relatively quickly, with occupational conversion for production workers in particular being quite straightforward, more time would be required for some development staff and administrative staff.[31] Support will also be necessary during the period needed to penetrate or create new markets; there must be an awareness of this, and explicit willingness to make proper provision for it.

In general, converted capacity should not enter competition with established British industries. This can be avoided by concentrating on fields of advanced technology in which British performance is now poor (or, in some cases, virtually non-existent). Alternatively, employees no longer required in military aerospace could be transferred to existing firms, who could receive development contracts from the Government through the NEB, to enable them to expand their expertise and markets. Established firms involved in this should be brought within the planning agreements system to establish full accountability.

It has already been pointed out that some of the alternative products involve basic decisions about major areas of government policy, decisions about, for example, boosting the National Health Service, developing new transport policy, entering profitable manufacture, how best to support newly converted capacity, relying on or turning away from nuclear power. There is a clear two-way relationship between these areas of policy and the potential for success in conversion and diversification of the arms industry.

In the nuclear power debate, for instance, a decision to rely on nuclear power would invalidate some of the most exciting conversion options available, although it could lead to another decision to utilize airframe experience to develop safer means of waste disposal. On the other hand, it is not permissible for the

132

decision about nuclear power to be taken without consideration of others means of power generation. Successful experiments with solar-powered generators, the development of the Nodding Duck wave-power system (see pp. 149-150) and the interest in both types of project shown by the South-West Energy Group and Harwell Energy Technology Support Unit make it impossible to dismiss 'alternative energy',[32] particularly when one realizes that the industrial capacity to develop these systems could be made available following arms cuts.

At no stage can consideration of conversion and diversification be divorced from other policy areas. The process will be anarchic and uncertain unless other policy is considered, and the proper planning undertaken.

Attitudes of the Workforce

A problem many people have pointed to is the attitude of the workforce. This, of course, brings us in a sense back to square one – views attributed to workers and trade unions are regularly used as an argument against arms cuts, normally as a way of avoiding rather than entering debate.

In fact, there does not generally seem to be opposition to conversion and diversification *per se*. Naturally enough there is opposition to redundancy, and to incompletely planned and conceived schemes which might go off at half-cock, causing redundancies in the long run. There is opposition to purchasing arms from abroad while capacity lies idle or under-used in Britain, and there is opposition to taking on work which is less well paid, less skilful and less interesting.

Clearly, however, with so many of the suggestions for alternative products coming from the workforce, the argument that workers are all against conversion or diversification just does not hold water.

There will, however, be opposition to arms cuts unless and until there are concrete alternatives to provide jobs. There is a great deal of suspicion of proposals for arms cuts at present; this should cause us no surprise in view of the present unemployment total, at a time when investment is falling in Britain, and when it seems that the Treasury has been allowed to get away with a policy of creating unemployment. This should provide us with a warning, first that arms cuts are only acceptable to many if they are linked with provision of other work. Secondly, we should be clear that what has emerged in the work of the Study Group is a set of proposals and possibilities which adequately demonstrate

133

the feasibility and desirability of conversion and diversification, but do not yet add up to a blueprint. We can say that such a plan is possible, and that it would make a valuable contribution to sorting out defence policy and many of our industrial and economic problems – but we cannot claim to have developed that plan. The discussion above has shown that a good deal of preliminary work is necessary – market surveys, systematic search for products, collection of fuller data, etc. – before a government could draw up such a plan. The conclusions and recommendations of the Study Group must include urging that preliminary work be now undertaken.

Restructuring the Industry

A consideration that frequently escapes the attention of those working in this field is the question of the kind of framework within which converted capacity would function. The preference here is for a complete overhaul of the structure of the industry to give it a new start; this would include taking it out of the hands of present management, changing management structures, rejigging development teams, introducing a limited number of new personnel at key points, and developing new methods of operation. We can identify two major reasons which make this task essential.

In military aerospace, and, indeed, throughout military industry, it is a basic tenet that each product should be better than the last. The main rationale for the introduction of replacement weapon systems is that the existing systems are obsolescent. Improvements are seen in terms of better performance, and not, significantly, in terms of cost-reducing production techniques or other economies. Improved performance means increased sophistication. Of course, there have been sound reasons for this; an attempt to fight the Battle of Britain with Sopwith *Camels* would have been ludicrous as well as unsuccessful, and the *Spitfires* and other fighters of the Second World War are now, rightly, museum pieces. Sophistication, however, carries with it the penalties of expanding industrial capacity and increased costs.[32]

This drive for improvement is not a recent phenomenon – it begins with the first development of military aircraft. It has, however, now created practices and industrial structures which confuse and distort decisions about defence policy, and which are incompatible with competitive civil manufacture. This is not to say that each new civil product benefits by being worse than

134

its predecessor, but an improved product may be one which is simpler to use, cheaper to produce and cheaper to buy, not one which is more sophisticated and so necessarily more expensive. The kind of cost increases we have seen in major weapon systems are not supportable in the civil field.[33] Furthermore, increased sophistication does not always produce a better final product; Tornado is an example of this, as is the American B-1 bomber – benefits can be illusory.

This leads us to the second point. Military industry is not really profitable or competitive in the normal sense of the term, particularly in Britain, where the aerospace industry in particular has been rationalized by reducing the number of firms involved, to reduce the cost of maintaining military industrial capacity. With military industry, government fixes profit levels; development is funded so that the corporations themselves need not make irretrievable investment; purchase of the completed product is guaranteed if it comes up to scratch, and often if it falls far short of scratch. If a government decides it needs a military industry, it has to support and maintain the capacity involved – especially the development capacity, the technological 'core' of the industry – and provide it with work. In this sense, whether or not private profit is gained as a result, military industry is really a public industry, maintained by the Government according to its definition of the public good. It may be argued that industry has to compete in the export field; even there, the Defence Sales Organization (and foreign counterparts for other countries' industry) helps out in every way possible.

Neither development nor management techniques in military aerospace are really suitable for competitive manufacture on an open market. On a very simple level, it cannot be assumed that people whose whole experience has been in fields where cost is little or no object and where increased sophistication must always be provided, can easily adapt themselves to a field where cost is all-important, and increased sophistication of the final product is but one of many relevant considerations. We are demanding different methods and techniques – a different ethos.

In diluted form, these problems also apply to diversified capacity. Although the Government would remain the main or sole purchaser of the non-military products, we would certainly not want to see costs of, for example, medical equipment spiralling upwards through unnecessary extra sophistication for marginal or illusory benefits.

There should, therefore, be a clear separation between con-

135

verted and retained capacity. Ideally this separation should be both administrative and physical – converted capacity should function in different buildings, or even on a different site if one were available. As well as enabling people to have more control over matters directly affecting their prosperity and well-being, and providing a fertile new source of ideas, industrial democracy would be a way of enforcing change in industrial structures, and introduce a sense of urgency into marketing and cost reductions. A body such as the NEB would need to supervise and check on much of the functioning of the new industry; industrial democracy could also provide a kind of internal check. It is not that management or development methods are inefficient in military aerospace (though by one set of criteria they certainly are), but that they are inherently unsuited in many respects to the kind of manufacture in which conversion would involve them; therefore, they must be changed and replaced by ones more suitable.

Conclusions

Despite the unlikelihood of Tornado cancellation, and despite limited data, it is valuable to consider other uses to which the resources involved in the project could be committed. We have concentrated on work which can utilize present skills and technology, and this particularly means fields of advanced and advancing technology.

There will undoubtedly be a requirement to retain some military aerospace capacity; maintenance of this capacity could be made cheaper through diversification, with the important benefit of producing worthwhile things during periods when aerospace capacity is not required to be in full operation. In addition, this would provide the workforce with greater security.

For both conversion and diversification we can identify useful work which could contribute, variously, to the balance of payments, to the basic strength of our economy and industry, and to public spending programmes. For several of the products, certain fairly basic decisions are required about other areas of policy. Adequate planning is a crucial part of the process, and this must be based on yet more preliminary work. If these alternatives are presented in a concrete and practical form, there is no reason to expect oppositon from the workforce involved in military aerospace. We shall, however, face real barriers to success unless conversion planning includes restructuring in the industry which is converted.

We can conclude that this planning task is possible, and that

136

the opportunity for a successful programme of conversion and diversification exists.

DAN SMITH

Notes and References
1. David Greenwood, 'Defence Programme Options to 1980/81', October 1975, for the Study Group.
2. *Hansard*, 18 March 1976, cols. 1627–53.
3. William Rodgers, MP, in ibid., col. 1650.
4. Both quoted in 'More Attacks on NATO Plane', *Sunday Times*, 3 October 1976.
5. Various estimates in the region of Mach 3 had been made before the Mig-25 was closely examined; it now appears that the machometer is 'redlined' at 2.8; see 'The Mig-25 Saga', *Air International*, November 1976.
6. See Defence and External Affairs Sub-committee of the Expenditure Committee, Minutes of 27 April 1976, House of Commons, 236-v, Questions 407–12.
7. Geoffrey Pattie, *Towards a New Defence Policy*, Conservative Political Centre, 1976, p. 16.
8. See 'Europe's F-16 Plans Unfold', *Flight International*, 23 October 1976.
9. 'The End of the MRCA?', in Ulrich Albrecht and others, *The Anti-White Book*, FRG, 1974.
10. W. B. Walker, 'The Multi-Role Combat Aircraft (MRCA): a Case-Study in European Collaboration', in *Research Policy*, 2, 1974, discusses the disadvantageous consequences of collaboration; William D. White, *U.S. Tactical Air Power*, Brookings Institution, Washington DC, 1974, discusses the relative merits of multi-role and specialized aircraft (pp. 55–9), and the changing strategic environment. The implications of this for British defence policy, and Tornado in particular, are discussed in Dan Smith, 'Strategic and Political Implications of Reduced Defence Programmes', May 1976, for the Study Group.
11. *Hansard*, 5 November 1975, and 17 December 1975.
12. See *Financial Times*, 10 October 1975.
13. For example, most recently, see 'Aerospace Decisions Now, EEC tells Britain', *Flight International*, 16 October 1976; it would appear that as far as there is British interest in civil aerospace collaboration, it is directed towards further bilateral collaboration with France, not towards EEC-wide projects.
14. Aircraft and Shipbuilding Industries Act 1977; see Part I, Clauses 2(5) and (6), and 3(1).
15. 'Lords Modify Nationalization Bill', *Flight International*, 23 October 1976.
16. Part I, Clause 2(8); see also Part I, Clauses 5(1), 7(1), and 8(2). (This paragraph has been drafted to replace two in the original paper which discussed the then uncertain future of the Bill.)
17. *Hansard*, 17 December 1975.
18. Roy Mason, MP, *Hansard*, 31 March 1976, col. 1334; at peak, a further 8,000 are expected to be employed on avionics and equipment, giving a total of 24,000 workers directly employed, with another 12,000 employed 'indirectly'.

19. See *Labour's Programme for Britain 1976*, chs. 2 and 3.
20. James J. McDonagh and Steven M. Zimmerman, 'Mobilization for Peace: A Program for Civilian Diversification of the Airframe Industry', unpublished thesis at Columbia University, 1961, p. 181.
21. *Buns Before Gutter*, discussion document for aerospace shop stewards, 1976; Peter Ward, *Alternatives to Arms Production*, paper for Preston Trades Council Day School, April 1976; Dan Smith, 'Aspects of Conversion of Arms Industries', January 1976 for the Study Group.
22. See Mary Kaldor, 'Alternative Employment for Naval Ship-building Workers: A Case-Study of the Resources Devoted to the Production of the ASW Cruiser', March 1976, for the Study Group. (Reprinted here as Case-study Two, Part 2, pp. 145-54.)
23. See n. 21 *supra*.
24. Dan Smith, 'Aspects of Conversion of Arms Industries', p. 11.
25. The USAF AMST programme for a STOL military transport involves two competing prototypes (Boeing's YC-14 and McDonnell Douglas's YC-15), both of which have flown; selection between them is expected in September 1977 for entry into service in 1983: see 'YC-14, All Blow and No Puff!', *Air International*, November 1976.
26. As n. 21 *supra*, pp. 13 and 15.
27. See *Labour's Programme for Britain 1976*, Ch. 3.
28. Peter Ward, paper cit.
29. ibid.
30. See Dan Smith, 'Community Planning and Base Conversion', November 1976, for the Study Group.
31. Dan Smith, 'Aspects of Conversion of Arms Industries', pp. 6–10.
32. See 'Million-Watt U.S. Solar Boiler is Tested in French Pyrenees', *International Herald Tribune*, 20 October 1976, and 'Second Chance for Solar Energy', *Guardian*, 1 November 1976.
32. For a full discussion of this process, see Mary Kaldor, 'European Defence Industries – National and International Implications', ISIO Sussex University, 1972, and 'Defence, Industrial Capacity and the Economy', March 1976, for the Study Group.
33. See Norman R. Augustine, 'One Plane, One Tank, One Ship: Trend for the Future?', *Defense Management Journal*, April 1975; the discussion there shows a remarkably steady increase in costs of all major weapons systems, and includes the calculations that if the trends continue, the entire US Department of Defense budget will be able to purchase only one aircraft in the year 2036!

(For information and other help in preparing this paper the author is grateful to the following: Bob Crook, David Griffiths, Brian Hesketh, Mary Kaldor and Peter Ward. Naturally none of them is responsible for the contents or conclusions of the paper.)

Two: THE ANTI-SUBMARINE
WARFARE (ASW) CRUISER

Part 1: Background to the Project

The Anti-Submarine Warfare (ASW) or through deck cruiser is a euphemism for 'small aircraft carrier'. The euphemism is required because the last Labour Government took the decision to phase out the British carrier force and to allocate all fixed-wing aircraft to the RAF. Lest the RAF be offended or thinking people be critical, the latest carrier is disguised as a cruiser.

The functions of the cruiser are twofold: (a) command, control and co-ordination of British and NATO maritime forces and (b) the deployment of ASW aircraft – the Sea King helicopter and the Harrier VTOL aircraft. The Ministry of Defence claims that to combine these functions in a single large hull is the most 'cost-effective' solution. There are, however, two fundamental weaknesses in their case. First, because all surface ships are vulnerable to attack from the air or from below the surface, a single 'cost-effective' solution in peacetime may prove an expensive disaster in war. The Ministry argue that 'the vulnerability of the cruiser will be no greater than that of any other ship in the force'. But to justify its expense the cruiser must be considerably less vulnerable. Secondly, it is not clear in what circumstances these functions will be carried out. The new naval scenario that has emerged since withdrawal from the Far East is the Battle of the Eastern Atlantic. So critical is this battle considered that only a few tugs could be spared for the defence

139

of North Sea Oil. The exact nature of the battle has not been defined. There is vague talk about providing a 'mix of naval forces with a capability across the whole spectrum of possible naval operations'. And the cruiser is described as a unit 'with a greater capability for operations at the higher level'. When a member of the Expenditure Committee asked if the planners were 'contemplating a war with an eastern bloc power which will go on long enough for us to be involved in convoy protection work and in the protection of amphibious forces crossing the channel', the Ministry of Defence witness produced a useful catch-all formula: 'We are contemplating a deterrent concept of operations at sea – a situation in which the Soviet fleet could be deployed to bring either military or political pressure to bear. NATO's concept of operations at sea is exactly parallel with its concept of operations on land.'[1]

This formula has emerged since the 1966 White Paper which envisaged that the tasks for carrierborne aircraft in the late 1970s could be 'more cheaply' performed in other ways.[2] In particular, anti-submarine protection would be given by helicopters operating from ships other than carriers, while early-warning aircraft would eventually operate from land bases. The cost of a carrier force was estimated at £1,400 million over ten years, hardly more than the estimate of £1,200 million for the planned cruiser force (see below).

Denis Healey, then Minister of Defence, explained the thinking behind this decision in a lecture to the Royal United Services Institute on 2 October 1969:

It was obviously necessary to see whether it was really essential to spend these enormous sums on so limited a capability. It emerged rapidly that the role of the carrier in support of land operations could in most places which concerned us, be carried out more cheaply and effectively by land-based aircraft; and that if we renounced the strategic option of landing or withdrawing troops against sophisticated opposition outside the range of friendly, land-based aircraft, this would have little important effect on our commitments. So the case for maintaining the carrier force depended critically on its role in maritime operations – a requirement which had been regarded up to then as simply a convenient by-product of the carriers' main role. This turned out to be a difficult nut to crack if one envisaged high-intensity maritime operations against a sophisticated enemy

140

in the Indian Ocean in the next decade. On the other hand the value of a single carrier on station in such operations was open to doubt. While it was a difficult judgement to decide against a carrier force for maritime operations East of Suez, once we had decided to withdraw from major military responsibilities in that area in the middle seventies I do not believe that the decision was easy to contest.

The decision to abandon carriers was not simply a decision to abandon carriers. It was a decision to abandon a sizeable chunk of the navy. Carriers are at the apex of the British naval structure. They justify the existence of the Fleet Air Arm, of a number of frigates and destroyers and hunter-killer submarines needed for protection, and of supply ships needed for replenishment. The navy would inevitably protest.

Almost as soon as the decision was taken, the case for small carriers was aired. (The idea had been mooted as far back as 1960.) 'Only if the Fleet Air Arm is deployed from a large number of carriers can it provide world-wide air cover; only if those carriers are small and simple can there be any hope of approaching the number needed . . . Nelson never had enough frigates either, but at least he did not have to contend with some economic genius intent on concentrating all his escort tonnage into three or four super frigates on the ground of cost-effectiveness.'[3] Healey was adamant in opposing the small carrier, but the notion was taken up almost as soon as the Conservatives took power in 1970. The new small carriers turned out to be three super frigates or cruisers, justified on grounds of cost-effectiveness. Conceptions of maritime operations were shifted from the Indian Ocean to the Eastern Atlantic, along with the all-embracing doctrine of 'flexible response'.

The change of heart was not simply due to the change of government, to the naval fantasies of Lord Carrington. There was considerable concern in 1971 and 1972 about excess naval capacity in the shipbuilding industry. In particular, the bankruptcy and work-in at Upper Clyde was followed by an accelerated naval building programme in Northern shipyards. In announcing the programme, the Minister of State for Defence Procurement made it clear that 'this was a special exercise to help not only the navy but employment'.[4] The lead items for the cruiser were ordered shortly afterwards. It was not only the shipbuilding industry that stood to gain; substantial orders for electronics, missiles and aircraft were also involved. For example, the cruiser is designed to operate the maritime Harrier. A number of prospective overseas customers informed the British Government that orders for the maritime Harrier were dependent on a British order.

The industrial aspects will be discussed in more detail in Part 2 (p. 145ff), but they may perhaps explain why the Labour Government has not found it possible to reverse the decision. For the strategic objections still remain. They were summarized by Vice-Admiral Sir Ian McGeogh:

Professional opinion, and especially that of experienced naval aviators, remains extremely sceptical of the wisdom of the TDC (Through Deck Cruiser) concept. It is pointed out that to combine in one ship the functions of Force flagship, area defence, anti-submarine helicoptership and fixed-wing V/STOL carrier is to ensure that none of these functions will be effective. In addition, the cost . . . will ensure that not more than three of them will be built. Furthermore, despite her size and armament, most of which, in any case, is defensive, such a ship would have no armoured protection and be just as vulnerable as any other to torpedo attack or mining. In action, she would inevitably be the main target for all kinds of attack and once damaged, let alone sunk, she would cease to be an asset to the Force Commander and become his biggest liability. Unlike the Cruiser, in its original environment, which could steam anywhere in safety, being fast enough to evade the only superior forces it might encounter, the TDC could not be safely allowed out of harbour in time of international tension or hostilities, without a screen of anti-submarine frigates at least. Her own helicopters would be quite inadequate, unassisted, to give the TDC reasonable anti-submarine protection.[5]

Cost

The table below is an estimate of the life-time cost of the cruiser programme at current prices, including the cost of associated equipment such as aircraft and protective vessels. (The cost of missiles, Sea Dart and Sea Wolf, is included in the basic cost of the cruiser and the frigates.)

	£m
Basic cost of 3 cruisers	390[6]
Basic cost of 25 Harriers	85[7]
Basic cost of 37 Sea Kings	83[8]
Basic cost of Support Ships (including Type 21 or Type 22 frigates, supply ships, a hunter killer submarine)	250–300[9]
Running cost of 3 cruisers (over 20-year lifetime)	320[10]
Running cost of support ships (over 20-year lifetime)	200[11]
Cost of associated shore personnel (over 20-year lifetime)	390[12]
Cost of aircraft spares (over 15-year lifetime)	168[13]
Cost of new aircraft (after 15 years)	336[14]
Cost of aircraft spares (over 5 years)	112
Total functional cost of cruisers over 20 years	2,360

Thus the cruisers will cost approximately £120 million a year. This is based on current estimates and does not take into account cost escalation, which inevitably occurs and has already occurred to some extent. The final cost may be as much as three times this figure, i.e. around £360 million a year.

MARY KALDOR

Notes and References

1. HCP 99-V111, Session 1973–4.
2. Statement on the Defence Estimates, 1966, Cmnd 2901 and 2902.
3. Lieutenant-Commander F. P. U. Croker, RN, 'David or Goliath? An Essay in Cost Effectiveness', *RUSI* Journal, May 1966.
4. House of Commons Report, 11 November 1971, col. 1228.
5. Ian McGeogh, *Command of the Sea in the Seventies*, The Waverly Papers, University of Edinburgh, Occasional Paper 1: Series 4.
6. A figure of £330 million for a classified number of cruisers was given in evidence to the Expenditure Committee, HCP 99-V111. It is widely assumed that the number is three since this is the minimum necessary to ensure that at least one cruiser is continuously in operation. £390 million allows for inflation.
7. Eight Harriers are needed for each ship, plus eight in reserve and one trainer. See *Flight*, 19 June 1975.
8. Nine Sea Kings are required for each ship. It is assumed that a further nine are kept in reserve, plus one for training purposes. The unit cost of Sea King is £2.25 million, according to the *Daily Telegraph*, 10 March 1975. (They may cost more if a fee for development work is included.)
9. Estimate, based on similar figures calculated for aircraft carriers in the 1960s (see Neville Brown, *New Scientist*, 27 January 1966), and on cost per ton of different kinds of ships calculated from *Jane's Fighting Ships* and other sources.

10. This is based on figures provided to the Expenditure Committee. They seem rather low. For example, personnel costs work out at around £1,500 per man. Yet the average cost in pay and allowances of the armed forces in general works out at £3,200 per man.
11. Estimate arrived at by extrapolating the running cost of the cruiser; it could, therefore, be low.
12. Estimate based on assumption of man ashore for every man on board ship.
13. Over the lifetime of an aircraft, spares are generally reckoned to cost roughly the same as the original acquisition cost.
14. Estimate based on conservative assumption that the next generation of aircraft will cost twice as much as the present generation. No sum is included to cover conversion of the cruiser to take new types of aircraft.

(The author is grateful to Paul Cockles and Major Elliott of the IISS for help in obtaining information for this paper.)

Part 2: Alternative Employment for Naval Shipbuilding Workers[1]

The ASW Cruiser is being built by the Vickers Shipbuilding Group at Barrow-in-Furness. The group employs around 13,000 workers and has an annual output of £64 million. The cruiser probably takes up about a fifth of Barrow's shipbuilding capacity and, over its lifetime, will involve around 7,000 to 8,000 man years of work. A further 28,000 to 32,000 man years will be taken up in the supplying industries – steel, marine equipment, etc.

The conversion problem, for all these people, is not so much technical as political. Any manner of alternative products could be made with the particular skills and talents, plant and facilities necessary for the production of the ASW Cruiser. The problem is the choice of products – a choice which depends on the local organization of the shipyard and its co-ordination with national policies towards industry, energy, transport, health, etc. This paper looks at both aspects of the problem. The first section deals with the people and resources employed at Barrow and the alternative production lines that have been suggested. The second section describes the contractor, Vickers Ltd, and why its current status and relationship with the Government must be changed if a successful conversion programme is to be carried out. The third section makes specific recommendations which are of relevance to the problem of defence conversion in general.

The conversion potential of the resources engaged in the pro-

145

duction of the ASW Cruiser is not just of particular interest. The Barrow shipyard is fairly typical of naval shipyards; the different requirements for submarines and smaller warships mainly concern the size of berths and the quantity of technical equipment. Equally, the problem of warship building conversion is not so different from the problem of finding work for surplus capacity in shipbuilding generally. Vickers Ltd is more than typical. If one includes its 40 per cent holding in BAC, it is the largest armaments company in Britain, producing the whole range of armaments from small-arms to ASW Cruisers and the Multi-Role Combat Aircraft. It is also an important multi-national company. In so far as its military and overseas divisions have expanded rapidly in recent years, while civilian British output has stagnated, it can be said to be typical not just of the armaments industry but of the British economy as a whole.

The Technical Problem of the Conversion: Alternative Products for Barrow Shipyard

The shipbuilding process, and the skills and facilities available at Barrow, are essentially commensurate with any kind of large-scale relatively labour-intensive construction and assembly activities which involve heavy metal fabrication and materials handling and complex logistical problems of supply, storage and scheduling. Preferably, alternative activities should be sea-based, partly because of the marine experience of the workers at Barrow, and partly because of the poor road and rail access to Barrow. Possible types of conversion can be broadly divided into three: merchant shipbuilding, alternative land-based manufacturing activities, and new sea-based technologies.

Merchant shipbuilding: The most obvious alternative activity, and the one preferred by boilermakers, is merchant shipbuilding. The Booz-Allen and Hamilton Report on British Shipbuilding 1972,[2] concluded that between £210 million and £250 million in new capital investment would be required to make British shipbuilding competitive. Clearly, much more would be required with today's recession in shipbuilding and today's price-level, but, even so, it is not a large sum when compared with the cost of three ASW Cruisers, i.e. £330 million. Furthermore, the UK has one advantage in the general shipbuilding gloom. The main collapse in shipping has occurred in the tanker market. Tankers are a relatively low proportion of total British output, and only Harland & Wolff have built the expensive capital-intensive

146

facilities needed for tanker production. The age of British plant and facilities could conceivably prove advantageous in the specialized markets of product carriers, container ships, etc., which are expected to dominate future orders.

Nevertheless, there is a strong case for arguing that money could be better spent in other ways, especially as regards the use of naval shipyards. First of all, there is tremendous over-capacity in shipbuilding. Industry spokesmen have estimated that, over the next ten years, world shipbuilding capacity will be twice world demand. This means that, in the excessive competition that can be expected, excessive amounts of money in terms of the social or economic return will be necessary to improve the UK competitive position. It also means that success in Britain will be at the expense of workers elsewhere. Secondly, the Barrow ship-yard is not the most appropriate for initiating such a competi-tive thrust. There are very expensive overheads to be borne and relatively large numbers of skilled labourers to be employed. Thus a naval shipyard typically employs twice as many salaried staff as a merchant shipyard, and a ship like the ASW Cruiser involves twice as many electricians and 50 per cent more boiler-makers than a passenger liner. Furthermore, test equipment is over-sophisticated, while craneage and steel handling facilities are inadequate because of lower weights of structural steel in warships.

It has been suggested that naval technology might have useful application to merchant shipbuilding in the future. Such ap-plications include nuclear propulsion, gas-turbine propulsion, or the use of lighter steel in merchant ships. It is likely that these ideas will prove to be too complex and expensive for commercial success. To take one example, the main advantage of gas-turbine propulsion is the ability to leave port in twenty minutes and to reach high speeds at sea rapidly. Few shipowners are likely to want these advantages in exchange for high cost, high fuel consumption and lack of tested reliability. Such problems are inherent to military technology. It is a mistake to confuse 'high' technology, which is costly and complex, like Concorde, with technology which is capable of serving socially useful ends and is likely, therefore, to be relatively cheap and simple.

Alternative land-based manufacturing activities: There is a large number of alternative technologies for which the skills and facilities available at Barrow are suitable. Indeed, both the shipbuilding and marine engineering group have manufactured

147

a wide range of products in the past. These include:

Cement kilns (using submarine technology)

Pumping plant and pipeline system for the Sadovia Corabia irrigation scheme in Romania

Sulzer diesel engines for British Rail during the changeover from steam to diesel engines

Sugar-beet crushers

Commercial boilers for power stations

Cable laying

Machinery for North Sea oil projects

Elsewhere, shipyards have been engaged in various kinds of construction activities, including watergates, locks, bridges, dams and even large buildings, structural steelwork, industrial machinery, including construction and mining equipment, metalworking machines and material handling equipment, and various kinds of transportation equipment. In some cases, as indeed for Vickers itself, these represented the post-war conversion routes. In others, they were merely means of filling excess capacity in the interim between naval or merchant-ship orders.

A study undertaken for the US Government identified fifty-five industries[2] suitable for conversion in the event of a one third cut in defence spending. The industries were chosen on the basis of two criteria: that they utilized similar skills and facilities, and that they would be relatively unaffected by defence cuts. It was found that, over a three-year period, one third of total naval building capacity could be converted by capturing 10 per cent of the annual *growth* of the market for these industries. Unfortunately, it has not yet been possible to calculate the growth of these industries in Britain. Although it is clear that, in the mid 1970s in Britain, the growth potential will be much smaller than in the United States in the mid 1960s, the American result indicates the scope of the conversion potential in this area.

In addition to existing industries, there is a whole range of new technologies being discussed that could prove suitable for Barrow. *Ad hoc* suggestions include:

Heat pumps: these are refrigerators in reverse, which draw in heat at low temperatures from water, soil or air and deliver it at a usefully high temperature. Particularly if it was combined with a solar collector, this could represent a relatively cheap and reliable method of home heating.

Solar panels

Containers

148

Prefabricated houses

Tanks for fish farming

Decompression chambers for hospitals

Pre-design bridges for disaster relief, etc.

Skips for cement

Recycling technologies, e.g. crushers, domestic refuse collection such as large drums for the production of high-quality compost

Fluidized bed boilers using pulverized coal for industry. These are small, portable and pollution-free

Heat exchangers: these are assemblies of pipes placed by boilers to collect waste heat

New kinds of energy-saving capital equipment, such as continuous casting for steel

Hover trucks

The main difficulty with these schemes is the existence of other factories or plants more appropriate for their development. Given the current unemployment in engineering generally, and the need to find conversion opportunities for the vehicles, ordnance and small-arms sectors, it would seem less appropriate to invest in Barrow where access is poor and marine experience would be wasted.

New sea-based technologies: it is widely considered that future developments in such fields as agriculture, mining, energy and transportation will be based on exploitation of the sea and the sea bed. As an island with considerable experience in sea-based technologies, Britain is in an ideal position to participate in these developments. Indeed, the greatest asset of our heavy naval building programme is the preponderance of naval designers. There are 3,200 people employed by the Ministry of Defence on R & D in warship construction. They cost £54 million, ten times as much as is spent on R & D into merchant shipbuilding. Although the technology developed by them in the past may have little immediate application, they represent a powerful creative force for new technologies in the future.

Possible ideas that might be developed at the Barrow shipyard are as follows:

Wave power: a wave-power generator has been designed by Stephen Salter of Edinburgh University. Known as the 'Nodding Duck', the generators are designed on exactly opposite principles from naval architecture, in order to rock as much as possible

149

with the waves. Each unit weighs 50,000 tons and is comprised of fifty smaller units, largely made from concrete, with hydraulics and electrics inside. Anchored across 300 miles of sea around the Hebrides, 100 units could provide sufficient power for the entire United Kingdom. Each unit would cost £10 million, would be labour-intensive to produce, employing very similar skills to shipbuilding. The test and design programme is ahead of schedule, and Dr Salter estimates that the generators will be ready to enter production in two years' time. The main problem is that of transmission to the main energy-using centres of Britain. Dr Salter and his colleagues have developed a scheme which, according to their estimates, will bring the cost of wave power to 1 to 1·2p per kilowatt hours, currently in the middle range of energy costs. Wave power is based on energy income rather than energy stocks and is therefore indefinite. It is also pollution free.

The main obstacle to wave power, as with the other energy projects listed below, is current energy requirements and policy. There is considerable over-capacity in electricity generation and this is estimated to reach 38 per cent by 1980. Furthermore, current pressures to preserve a coal industry, as well as from the oil and nuclear energy lobbies, put wave power, together with tidal power, at the bottom of the list of current energy priorities.

Tidal power: the main proposal for tidal power currently under consideration is the Severn Barrage. It is estimated that the barrage could provide one fifth of the energy consumed in the UK. This site has been chosen largely because of the existence of a local pressure group and an enthusiastic local MP. In fact, because of its effects on Bristol port and on holiday beaches, the Severn Estuary might not prove to be the most suitable site. Another suggestion is the Morecambe Barrage, which would, of course, be ideal for Barrow. It would involve very suitable large-scale construction technology.

Ocean thermal gradients: this would involve large condensers and evaporators designed to tap the temperature difference between deep and surface waters in the tropical seas. There are enormous transmission problems and the scheme would not be suitable for Britain. However, it might be possible for the Barrow shipyard to participate in schemes currently being proposed in the United States.

Submersibles for firefighting on oil rigs, nodule collection on the sea bed, deep-sea mining and marine agriculture. Clearly, these are ideal for Barrow, with its long experience in submarine

150

manufacture. Vickers Offshore Engineering, which has recently been detached from the shipbuilding group, is at the forefront of this technology with its fleet of five submersibles.

Ocean-going tub-barge system: barges that could be used at sea as well as on Britain's neglected canal system could be of particular use to Barrow in improving its communications with the rest of the UK. More generally, this kind of system – a sort of water-based lorry – could greatly ease cargo handling facilities and road and rail traffic. A related suggestion is a container barge.

River power: low-head, low-pressure turbines could be used to tap stream flows and deliver just a few kilowatts. Such a scheme, which would be suitable for development by the marine engineering group, would have enormous scope for villages in the Third World.

Other suggestions for new sea-based technologies include various types of deep-sea mining and farming equipment, modules covering the superstructure of drilling rigs, catamaran container ships, sea-skimmers for dealing with oil pollution, etc.

These projects will probably yield at least as much foreign exchange as our current expenditure on armaments. Currently, we export around a quarter of our total arms production, which is rather low compared with manufacturing generally, where the share of exports is one third. It seems unlikely that these new technologies, which have in any case an immediate social benefit, should generate directly or indirectly, through the general effect on the British economy, fewer exports than the average manufacturing activity.

The Political Problem of Conversion: Vickers Ltd

In a sense, the history of Vickers is a history of attempts at conversion. Vickers, originally a steel company, became a manufacturer of armaments and armour plate in the 1880s, and from there diversified into shipbuilding, marine engineering, steel and other component supplies. After each war, Vickers Ltd has attempted to adjust to peacetime conditions by expanding into such diverse areas as power presses, medical engineering, optical instruments, lithographic plates and supplies, bottling machinery, etc. It is only since the mid 1960s, when the steel business was nationalized and the company bought printing machinery and office equipment, that these efforts at diversification were successful.

The period coincided with increased overseas expansion by

151

the company. Over the last ten years, overseas sales have increased much faster than exports. In 1965, overseas sales were roughly twice the size of exports. In 1974, they exceeded exports by a factor of three. In particular, the company acquired a number of subsidiaries in Europe for the manufacture of office equipment (the Roneo Vickers group), and chemical engineering (the Howson-Algraphy group). In 1974, British acquisitions by the company amounted to £790,000, while foreign acquisitions in Australia and Sweden amounted to £2,310,000.

This policy will be continued after the nationalization of the shipbuilding group. The armaments and naval shipbuilding division, together with the overseas subsidiaries, are the only sections of Vickers to show continued growth and profitability. The prospects for British civilian establishments are considered poor. Leeds Water Lane factory, which manufactures newspaper printing machinery, is threatened with closure. The engineering factories at Otley, Scotswood, Elswick and South Marston are all on short time of one kind or another. Other factories, in engineering and lithographic plate, are threatened with short time.

The Chairman of Vickers, Lord Robens, has already implied his intention to spend the compensation monies abroad. In his Annual Report he wrote:

A large part of Vickers' activities in the United Kingdom will . . . continue without interruption, and in addition to the Engineering Group, Howson-Algraphy Group, Offshore Engineering and Vickers Instruments, we have extensive and successful operations in Australia and Canada. It will be the Board's first priority in use of compensation monies to add to the strength of these activities, whether by internal investment or by acquisition.

One British division which might benefit is the Offshore Engineering Group which, presumably to avoid nationalization, has recently been detached from the Shipbuilding Group, where it resided, according to the Chairman, 'for reasons of administrative convenience, though not engaged in shipbuilding'.[3]

Diversification through overseas expansion of Vickers makes sense on the criterion of private profit. It is, of course, a self-reinforcing policy since it contributes to the low level of investment in Britain and further limits the prospects for domestic diversification. In addition, the direction of such investment as does occur in Britain is dependent on the overall structure of British industry and reinforces current industrial trends. Thus the success of the Offshore Engineering Group reflects the fact that the oil industry is one of the few growth areas in Britain and, at the same time, creates a vested interest in further growth.

Nearly all the alternative projects described above are dependent on a high level of investment in Britain and a reversal of current industrial trends. The energy projects depend on an increased demand for electricity and a reversal of the current emphasis on oil and nuclear power. The transportation projects depend on the level of external and internal trade and a reversal of the current emphasis on road transportation, itself a reflection of the power of motor-car manufacturers and road constructors. The projects involving mining, marine agriculture and various kinds of capital equipment depend directly on the levels of investment and income and may also involve less emphasis on oil technology.

Recognition that the Government must enter industry as an investor is implicit in the nationalization of shipbuilding. But, by itself, it is insufficient to ensure a successful programme of conversion. We have seen in the past how nationalization has been used as a tool for the orderly contraction of declining industries. This is made possible by the preservation of existing organizational structures where local employees have little opportunity to make their views felt and where the direction of central government policy remains largely unchanged. Especially where the growing sectors of the industry, e.g. offshore engineering, are excluded from the nationalization, this kind of approach can be justified by the lack of alternative investment opportunities.

Conclusions

The following recommendations emerge from this survey of conversion potential of Barrow shipyard.

1. While alternative technologies could be enumerated, the most attractive opportunities lie in the development of new sea-based technologies, of which the best prospects are wave-power, submersibles and other equipment for nodule collection, mining and agriculture on the sea bed, and ocean tug-barge systems. There is no reason to suppose that the export potential of these projects would be less than that of armaments.

2. If these opportunities are to be exploited, the Government must:

(a) Enter the industry as a direct investor. Development contracts for new technologies are an essential and immediate alternative to defence spending or unemployment.

(b) Coordinate investment in these areas with other related policies such as energy, transport, health, agriculture, etc.

3. The Government can only act as an investor and reverse the direction of existing policies if current organizational structures are changed. This involves:

(a) Nationalization of some sectors of the defence industry, including the profitable civilian sectors, such as offshore engineering.

(b) Workers' participation in the nationalized industries, in order to generate ideas for alternative products and shift the central direction of government policymaking; i.e. wave-power is unlikely to be adopted by a government committed to oil and nuclear power. (An additional consideration is safety. For example, the need to improve the safety of submersibles and to reduce the problem of fuel extraction in shipbuilding might receive greater emphasis.)

(c) Planning agreements with all private armaments companies, in order to ensure that capacity freed from armaments production and that profits from armaments (which are currently high because of the practice of cost-plus contracting) and compensation monies from nationalization are invested in suitable projects in Britain rather than abroad.

MARY KALDOR

Notes and References
1. This paper was written in March 1976 and has not been updated.
2. *British Shipbuilding 1972.* A report to the Department of Trade and Industry by Booz-Allen and Hamilton International BV. HMSO, 1973.
3. *Final Report on Industrial Conversion Potential in the Shipbuilding Industry.* For US Arms Control and Disarmament Agency, Mid-West Research Institute Contract No. ACDA/E-66. MRI Project 2833-D. 18 March 1966.
4. Vickers Limited Annual Report and Accounts 1974.

(The author is grateful to Albert Booth, the shop-stewards of Barrow and the Vickers Shop-stewards Combine Committee who provided the basic material for this paper.)

154

APPENDIX ONE: A LIST OF PAPERS SUBMITTED TO THE NEC STUDY GROUP ON DEFENCE EXPENDITURE, THE ARMS TRADE AND ALTERNATIVE EMPLOYMENT

All papers were prepared for the Study Group unless stated. Papers are listed in order of presentation.

* Past member of the Defence Study Group.
† Paper published elsewhere.

The Extent of Defence Cuts
The Financial Implications of the Party's Commitment on Defence Expenditure – Office
Military Expenditure: Gross Domestic Product in NATO Europe – F. Blackaby
* Observations on the Proposal to Align UK Defence Expenditure with the Average Percentage Spent on Defence by the FRG, Italy and France – P. Cockle
Note on Military Expenditure and National Product: UK and Certain Other Countries – F. Blackaby
* Impact of Recent Changes in Italian Defence Expenditure on the Study Group's Assumption of the Average European Defence Burden – P. Cockle
* The Equi-Burden Calculation: 1975 Figures – P. Cockle

How Cuts Could Be Made
A Note on Approaches to Cutting Defence Spending – M. Kaldor and D. Smith

155

Defence Programme Options to 1980–81 – D. Greenwood
* Note on the Budget Approach and a Programme Option
Which Retains the UK Nuclear Strategic Force – P. Cockle

Defence Expenditure and the Economy
Defence, Industrial Capacity and the Economy – M. Kaldor
The Employment and Other Economic Consequences of Reduced
Defence Spending – D. Greenwood
The Resource Cost of Military Expenditure – R. P. Smith
† Military Expenditure, Exports and Growth – K. W. Rothschild,
Kyklos, vol. xxvi, 1973
Defence Cuts and the Defence Industry – M. Kaldor
The Opportunity Costs of Defence – M. Kaldor

The Strategic and Political Implications of Defence Cuts
† New Weapons Technologies and European Security – R.
Burt, *Orbis*, Summer 1975
† Defence Review: An Anti-White Paper – R. Cook, D. Holloway,
M. Kaldor and D. Smith, *Fabian Research Series*, November
1975
*Defence Programme Options to 1981: Politics – Strategic and
Economic Implications – A. L. Williams
Strategic and Political Implications of Reduced Defence Pro-
grammes – D. Smith
The Political and Strategic Consequences of a Cut in British
Military Expenditure – F. Blackaby
A Political Approach to Defence Cuts – D. Holloway and M.
Kaldor
Is There a Russian Threat? – R. Neild (talk presented to the
group)

Creating New Jobs
† The Clyde Submarine Base and the Local Economy – Timothy
Stone and David Greenwood, paper presented to the Scottish
CND Conference, 15 February 1975
The Multi-Role Combat Aircraft (MRCA) – D. Smith
The Anti-Submarine Warfare Cruiser – M. Kaldor
Note on the Employment Consequences of a £1,000 Million Cut
(at 1974 prices) in Military Expenditure Over Five Years – F.
Blackaby
† Arms, Jobs and the Crisis – *CND*, July 1975
* The Crisis in the Capital Goods Industry – A. Doll-Steinberg

Military Expenditure Cuts: Note on the Transfer of Resources – F. Blackaby
Aspects of Conversion of Arms Industries – D. Smith
† Corporate Plan – Lucas Aerospace Combine Shop Stewards Committee
Alternative Employment for Naval Shipbuilding Workers: A Case-study of the Resources Devoted to the Production of the ASW Cruiser – M. Kaldor and A. Booth
TORNADO – Cancellation, Conversion and Diversification in the Aerospace Industry – D. Smith
Community Planning and Base Conversion – D. Smith
Correspondence Relating to Vickers Oceanics – A. Booth and E. Varley

The Arms Trade
* Defence Exports: Some of the Benefits to the British Defence Effort and Economy – A. L. Williams
Defence and the Arms Trade – R. F. Cook
First Steps Towards Limiting Arms Transfers – S. Merritt
British Armaments Sales Abroad – F. Allaun
US Disclosure of Information on Defence Exports – J. Gilbert

APPENDIX TWO: A LIST OF PRODUCTS IDENTIFIED AS BEING SUITABLE FOR MANUFACTURE IN THE CONVERTED DEFENCE INDUSTRIES

In the following list, based on the material collected by the NEC's Defence Study Group, a large number of alternative products have been suggested. This list draws together the major proposals. It is not an exhaustive list, but it shows the kind of practical possibilities which could be realized if a planned conversion from military production were to take place. Some of the products listed are obviously of less importance than others, and their inclusion in this list does not suggest that there is automatically a possibility of direct conversion from military production. The purpose of this list is therefore, to show the scope and volume of opportunities which exist.

AEROSPACE AND RELATED MILITARY INDUSTRIES

Aircraft
Short- to medium-range civil aircraft seating up to 200
Civil helicopters to service North Sea oil installations
Short take-off and landing passenger and freight aircraft
Helium airships for air freight
Robot helicopter for crop spraying

Marine Vessels
Jet propulsion of ships
Submerged production systems

159

Micro-processors for submersibles
Marine mineral exploitation and marine agriculture

Transport
Retarder brake system for trains and coaches
Development of other brake systems for all vehicles
Speed/distance related warning systems
Battery cars
New rolling stock
Monorail development
Hybrid engines containing internal combustion engine,
    generator, batteries, electric motor

Energy
Nuclear material disposal
Integrated energy systems
Components for low-energy heating (e.g. solar heating)
Fuel-cell power plants
Standby power units for the computer industry
Power packs for oil pumping
Processing plants (e.g. sewage, proteins from fine chemicals,
    ethylene recovery from oil, etc.)
Barrage schemes (tidal power)
Extended application of gas-turbine systems

Medical
Pacemakers and renal dialysis machines
Medical electronic equipment, including hospital
    communications, computers in hospitals, etc.
Personalised machinery for the disabled.
Telecheiric machines

Building
Industrial soundproofing
Prefabricated parts for building

Mechanical Engineering
Ball screws and machine tools to produce them
Computer controlled servo-hydraulically operated machine tools
Other digitally controlled machine tools

Motors
Linear motors operating pumps and compressors
High-speed motors

Other
Electronic libraries
Self-teaching devices
Mechanized agricultural equipment
Test facilities for manufactured products

SHIPBUILDING AND RELATED MILITARY INDUSTRIES
Fabricated Structural Metals
Metal doors, sash, frames, etc.
Fabricated plate work
Sheet-metal work
Architectural metal work
Miscellaneous metal work

Railroad equipment
Locomotives
Railroad cars

Construction and Mining Machinery
Construction machinery and equipment
Mining machinery and equipment
Oilfield machinery and equipment

Special Industrial Machinery
Food products machinery
Textile machinery
Woodworking machinery
Paper industries machinery
Printing trades machinery
Other special industry machinery
Marine agriculture machinery

Materials Handling Equipment
Elevators
Conveyors
Hoists, cranes, monorails
Industrial trucks, etc.

161

Trailers and Miscellaneous Transportation Equipment
Truck trailers
Trailer coaches
Miscellaneous transportation
Pipe-laying barges
Semi-submersible oil-rigs

General Industrial Machinery and Equipment
Pumps, compressors and equipment
Blowers and fans
Industrial patterns
Mechanical power-transmission equipment
Industrial process furnaces and ovens
Other general industrial machinery

Service Industry Machines
Automatic merchandizing machines
Commercial laundry machines
Refrigerators and air-conditioners
Automated stockholding and issuing systems
Other service industry machines

Farm Machinery
Farm machinery and equipment

Metalworking Machinery
Metal-cutting machinery
Metal-forming machinery
Special dies, tools, jigs
Machine-tool accessories
Miscellaneous metalworking machinery
Telecheiric devices for metal-bearing nodules

Furniture and Fixtures
Public building furniture
Wood office furniture
Metal office furniture

Others
Machine shops, jobbing and repair
Iron and steel forgings
Castings and engravings
Turbines and steam engines

162

Internal combustion engines
Electrical measuring instruments
Non-electrical heating equipment
Steel springs
Other fabricated metal products
Screw machine products
Bolts, nuts, screws

CHECK-LIST OF PAPERS TO BE INCLUDED IN THE APPENDICES OF THE FORTHCOMING EXTENDED EDITION OF THIS BOOK

NOTE: The criteria for inclusion in this list is that the papers have been referred to in the text. Papers not included have been substantially incorporated into the main part of the text itself. Appendices III to XVII can be purchased separately in pamphlet form from: Literature Sales Department, The Labour Party, Transport House, Smith Square, London SW1P 3JA. Those marked (*) will be available only in the forthcoming extended edition.

Appendix I: Papers Submitted to the Defence Study Group, etc.

Appendix II: Products Identified as Suitable for Manufacture in the Converted Defence Industries

Appendix III: Observations on the Proposal to Align UK Defence Expenditure with the Average Percentage Spent on Defence by the FRG, Italy and France – P. Cockle

Appendix IV: Note on the Military Expenditure and National Product: UK and Certain Other Countries – F. Blackaby

Appendix V: Defence Programme Options to 1980–81 – D. Greenwood (plus postscript)

Appendix VI: Note on the Budget Approach and a Programme Option which Retains the UK Nuclear Strategic Force – P. Cockle

Appendix VII: The Employment and Other Economic Consequences of Reduced Defence Spending – D. Greenwood (plus postscript)

165

Appendix VIII: The Resource Cost of Military Expenditure –
R. P. Smith

Appendix IX: Defence Cuts and the Defence Industry – M.
Kaldor

Appendix X: Defence Programme Options to 1981: Politico-
Strategic and Economic Implications – A. L. Williams

Appendix XI: Strategic and Political Implications of Reduced
Defence Programmes – D. Smith

Appendix XII: Note on the Employment Consequences of a
£1,000m Cut (at 1974 Prices) in Military Expenditure Over 5
Years – F. Blackaby

Appendix XIII: Military Expenditure Cuts: Note on the Transfer
of Resources – F. Blackaby

Appendix XIV: Aspects of Conversion of Arms Industries – D.
Smith

Appendix XV: Alternative Employment for Naval Shipbuilding
Workers: A Case-study of the Resources Devoted to the
Production of the ASW Cruiser – M. Kaldor and A. Booth

Appendix XVI: Tornado – Cancellation, Conversion and
Diversification in the Aerospace Industry – D. Smith

Appendix XVII: Community Planning and Base Conversion –
D. Smith

* Appendix XVIII: A Case-study in the Resources Devoted to
the Production of the Chieftain Tank – M. Kaldor

* Appendix XIX: A Summary of the Lucas Aerospace Corporate
Plan – M. Cooley

Appendix XX: British Arms Sales
   (a) Major Weapons Systems to Third World and Industrialized
      Countries
   (b) Licensed Production of British Arms Abroad
   (c) British Production of Major Weapons System
      (CAAT – Fact Sheets)

ALSO AVAILABLE IN PAMPHLET FORM:

Study into Defence Spending: Summary of Conclusions – John
Gilbert, James Wellbeloved and John Tomlinson

The Industrial and Employment Implications of Changing from
Defence to Civil Production – Les Huckfield